Library Use Only

Library Use Only

Rourke's Native American History & Culture
ENCYCLOPEDIA

Volume 4
Fox to Indian Territory

By Julie K. Lundgren

Project Consultant
Scott Lyons Ph.D.

Rourke
Publishing LLC
Vero Beach, Florida 32964

On The Cover

Detail from a painting by Karl Bodmer, 1809-1893

Tepee in Alberta, Canada

Zuni girl photographed by Edward S. Curtis, 1903

Anasazi cliff dwelling in Mesa Verde National Park, Colorado

Project Consultant
Scott Lyons Ph.D., an Ojibwe from Leech Lake, teaches at Syracuse University. He is also a columnist for *Indian Country Today*, a Native American on-line and print publication.

www.rourkepublishing.com

Photo credits: Cover Photos - © V. J. Matthew, © John S. Sfondilias, and Library of Congress; Page 4 - Karl Bodmer; Page 6 © George Catlin; Pages 8 - Courtesy of Library of congress; Page 10 - Library of Congress Civil War Collection; Page 11 © SalomonCeb; Page 12 - Courtesy of Library of Congress, Page 13b © Wmpearl; Page 14 © Leo Kowal; Pages 15, 16 - Courtesy of Library of Congress; Page 17 - Edward S. Curtis Collection (Library of Congress); Page 18 - Courtesy of Library of congress; Page 20 © Ra'ike; Page 21 - National Archives and Records Administration; Page 22 - Edward S. Curtis Collection (Library of Congress); Page 23 © Ryan Bushby; Page 24 - Courtesy of Library of congress; Page 26 © Raphaelle Peale; Page 27 - Edward S. Curtis Collection (Library of Congress); Page 28 - Courtesy of Library of congress; Page 29 © Bryan Brazil; Page 29b © Gary Blakeley; Pages 30, 31, 32, 33, 34 - Courtesy of Library of congress; Page 35 © Suzanne Long; Page 35b © Ivan Cholakov; Page 36 - Courtesy of Library of Congress; Page 37 © MWaits; Pages 38, 40, 41 Courtesy of Library of Congress; Page 42 © Winthrop Brookhouse; Page 43 - PCL Map Collection at the University of Texas Libraries; Page 43b © Nmajdan; Page 44 - Courtesy of Library of Congress; Page 44b - The University of South Dakota, 1975, "From the Collection of the University of South Dakota"; Page 45 - Edward S. Curtis Collection (Library of Congress); Page 46 - Courtesy of Library of Congress; Page 46b © David P. Lewis; Page 47 - Courtesy of Library of Congress; Page 47b - Edward S. Curtis Collection (Library of Congress); Pages 48, 51, 52 - Courtesy of Library of Congress; Page 54 © Nikater

Also, the author thanks historian Mark J. Johnston

Editor: Meg Greve

Cover and page design by Nicola Stratford

Library of Congress Cataloging-in-Publication Data

Volume 4 of 10
Set ISBN 978-1-60472-421-9

Printed in the USA

CG/CG

Rourke Publishing

www.rourkepublishing.com – rourke@rourkepublishing.com
Post Office Box 3328, Vero Beach, FL 32964

In 1492 Christopher Columbus sailed from Europe to North America and changed the world forever. Soon people from crowded European cities learned of the New World — a big, beautiful place where they could hunt, farm, and worship in freedom. For the millions of people already living there, however, this world was not new, it was home.

Their ancestors had been living on the American continents for thousands of years. They had their own rich civilizations, languages, and cultures. Columbus called them Indians, thinking he had reached India. Today, in the United States, they are called Native Americans and in Canada they are called First Peoples. They are further categorized by their tribal names, such as Cherokee, Mohawk, or Hopi.

Translated into English, many tribal names simply mean *The People*. As this name implies, they were the people of the land, the only people. Then Europeans came to North America. Colonists settled the eastern coast of North America and later established the United States. Then pioneers arrived and moved to new areas, west of the colonies. The incoming Europeans brought a hunger for more land. They also brought diseases, for which the Native Americans had no immunity.

During a period of four hundred years after the arrival of Columbus, both the Native Americans and the settlers faced immense challenges. During this time, millions of Native Americans died from disease and war. Since the 1900s, however, their populations have grown and much of their culture has survived. This encyclopedia series presents significant people and events in the history of Native Americans from the arrival of the Europeans to present-day events.

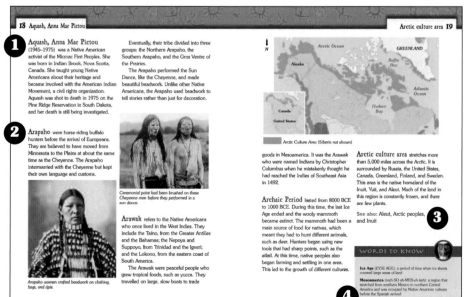

1. People are listed with their last name first.
2. The entries reference over 200 Native American tribes. They are listed by their most familiar name. A pronunciation chart is provided for many of the tribe names on page 64.
3. Cross-references direct you to additional information related to a topic.
4. "Words to Know" glossary is embedded in the text to help you pronounce and understand unfamiliar words.

Karl Bodmer painted this Fox man in the 1840s.

Fox (also known as Mesquaki, Mesquakie, and Meskwaki, meaning *red earth people*) people lived in the western Great Lakes region in the area of today's Wisconsin in the early 1700s. They lived near both prairie and forest. The Fox tribe followed the seasons. In summer, they constructed houses with wooden pole frames covered in bark. They farmed the woodland river valleys, planting beans, corn, squash, pumpkins, and tobacco. In winter, they hunted bison, also called buffalo, and other game, moving their camps as needed to follow the herds. In ceremonies, the Fox smoked tobacco in a calumet, a special pipe. Pipe smoking held deep meaning for the Fox people, for the ritual had the power to bring peace, show respect, and cement ties to other groups. After the Fox War, the tribe moved west of the Mississippi River. Today, tribal lands and reserves in Iowa, Kansas, and Oklahoma serve as their homes.

See also: Sac

Fox War, part of the French and Indian Wars, involved the French, Dakota Sioux, and Ojibwe against the Fox people from 1712 to 1737. The French had fur trade interests in the area and traded with the Fox and other Algonquian tribes. Unlike most neighboring tribes, when the French and British began to war against each other, the Fox took up arms against the French. Their long time enemies, the Ojibwe, sided with the French, and the Fox would not fight on the same side as the Ojibwe. The Fox also charged the French tolls for passage on the Fox River. Through this war, the French and Ojibwe gained control of Fox lands.

Freedmen refer to former slaves freed by the Emancipation Proclamation of 1865. Prior to the start of the Civil War in 1861, native peoples in the Five Civilized Tribes, including the Seminole, Creek, Chickasaw, Choctaw, and Cherokee, owned about 10,000 African slaves. After the Emancipation Proclamation, the U.S. government required slaveholders to free their slaves and give them full citizenship or face penalties.

French and Indian War, also known as the Seven Years' War, involved the British and the French. Both sides used Native American tribes to help them. In 1756, after two years of scattered fighting, the British formally declared war on the

French. Both the British and French wanted to claim lands, particularly the land between the Appalachian Mountains and the Mississippi River. This land held rich animal resources important in the fur trade. The colonists joined the fighting because of the belief that whoever won the war would force their religion on the losers. Late in the war, the Spanish joined the French against the British. The British won. In 1763, the signing of the Treaty of Paris ended the war. The British received all French lands east of the Mississippi River, some lands in Canada, and Spanish Florida. France gave Spain its holdings in French Louisiana to make up for Spain's loss of Florida. After this, France owned very little land in North America.

Tribes carved wampum beads from shells.

French peace wampum belt refers to a ceremonial piece made by Iroquoian tribes like the Haudenosaunee, or Iroquois nations, to mark important peace agreements between their tribes and the French. French fur traders actively pursued agreements with native peoples. They wanted access to the land and labor the Algonquian tribes could provide. For the Haudenosaunee, wampum belts expressed faith and kinship between peoples. It meant they would honor the agreement.

See also: wampum

Gabrieleño

Gabrieleño (also known as Gabrielino and Tongva) people lived near the Pacific coast of North America, in the region of today's Los Angeles, California, including Santa Catalina Island. They spoke a Uto-Aztecan language before the Spanish arrived in the area. When the Spanish brought Christianity and set up missions, people began calling the tribes by the name of the closest mission, in this case the Mission San Gabrielino. The Gabrieleño built houses with pole frames covered by reed mats or sealskins. Whale ribs sometimes replaced the poles. The Gabrieleño hunted small game, fished, and gathered acorns and edible plants. Settlement by outsiders from Mexico and the East, and outbreaks of disease, led to the tribe's near extinction by about 1900. Descendants, with headquarters today at San Gabriel, California, strive for federal recognition as a tribe.

WORDS TO KNOW

claim (KLAYM): to declare ownership

game (GAYM): birds and fur-bearing animals hunted for food

kinship (KIHN-ship): bonds or family ties

Gadsden Treaty, or Gadsden Purchase, signed between Mexico and the U.S. in 1853, settled border arguments after the Mexican-American War. The U.S. wanted a southern rail route connecting the East with the West. James Gadsden, who owned shares in the railroad picked to build the line, negotiated the treaty with Mexico. The Gadsden Treaty made changes in the Treaty of Guadalupe Hidalgo, the original peace agreement after the war. Gadsden promised ten million dollars for southern New Mexico and Arizona. Though the U.S. only delivered six million dollars, Mexico bitterly agreed to the treaty to avoid a renewal of a war they could not afford. This bitterness and mistrust lasted for many years.

Gall, (1840-1894) (also known as Pizi, meaning *man who goes in the middle*) was a Hunkpapa Lakota chief whose name refers to his fearlessness in battle. He led warriors in Red Cloud's War and in 1868 signed the Treaty of Fort Laramie to end it. In 1876, Chiefs Sitting Bull, Gall, and Crazy Horse, led warriors to victory at Little Bighorn. Gall followed Sitting Bull to Canada, but later returned to the U.S., settling on the Standing Rock Reservation in Dakota Territory, preferring to farm in peace instead of continued war.

See also: Little Bighorn, Battle of and Sitting Bull

Games of athletic skill and chance were popular in Native American life. Every tribe had its own variations of games. In hoop-and-pole, players tried to toss or slide a pole through a rolling, netted hoop. California Indians like the Maidu, and Plains peoples like the Hidatsa, passed the time with this game.

The game of lacrosse went beyond just having fun. It served as a kind of medicine to bring players and nations a sense of well-being. It settled arguments that could not be resolved by discussion. The winner of the game also won the argument. Many tribes played lacrosse, including the Iroquois tribes, the Cherokee, Creek, Choctaw, California Indians, and Santee Sioux.

Native American lacrosse games sometimes involved hundreds of players.

The Inuit played a kind of soccer keep-away with a leather ball stuffed with caribou hair. Unlike soccer, kicking goals wasn't the object of this game. Instead, a

Native Americans made game balls out of stone, clay, wood, or animal skin stuffed with hair.

team won by keeping control of the ball the longest. Kutchin athletes participated in wrestling matches. Again, a chief might suggest a wrestling match to settle a disagreement between two tribesmen. Games sometimes prepared players for adult life, such as battle games like the Mandan played. Mandan boys split into two teams, each coached by an experienced warrior. They practiced battle moves and strategies, and then held a battle game.

For the Choctaw, highly competitive song contests among villages of the same tribe entertained everyone. Many tribes enjoyed indoor games, such as a string game similar to cat's cradle, dice games, and betting. Players made dice out of wood, stone, bone, shell, and even seeds. Gamblers bet on running races or horse races in addition to guessing games and other games of chance.

See also: batey and lacrosse

General Allotment Act of 1887,

also known as Dawes Allotment Act, ordered the division of reservation lands to Native Americans in 160-acre (64-hectare) shares. According to the law, heads of households would receive the land. The United States government could sell any leftover land. Supporters of the act claimed it would force Native Americans to assimilate into mainstream American culture by moving them from community landholding to individual ownership. The main result of the act, however, was to strip Native Americans of much of their land and ruin them financially. The law held until 1934 when Congress passed the Indian Reorganization Act.

Genocide is the intentional murder of a

certain category of people, particularly those of a certain race or set of beliefs. Cultural genocide means erasing a way of life. Throughout history, Native American culture including language, the importance of community, spiritual practices and beliefs, and clothing and shelter, was constantly under attack.

WORDS TO KNOW

assimilate (uh-SIHM-uh-layt): to blend in with the surrounding ruling culture

negotiate (nuh-GOH-shee-ayt): to bargain or talk over problems in order to come to an agreement

George, Chief Dan (1899-1981) was the leader of the Salish people of British Columbia from 1951 to 1963. Though he did not begin his acting career until he was 60 years old, he played roles in many films and won an Academy Award nomination for his role in the movie *Little Big Man*. He attempted to promote understanding of First Nations peoples' beliefs and values and wrote several books on that subject.

Meet Geronimo

Geronimo (1829-1909) (also known as Goyakla and Goyathlay, meaning *one who yawns*) acted as a Chiricahua Apache military and spiritual leader in the American Southwest. He rose to power in the 1870s during the last efforts of the western native peoples to keep their traditional lands. The United States Army, with support from pioneers and Mexicans, pushed the Chiricahuas onto the San Carlos Reservation in southeastern Arizona territory, an area of harsh desert. Those who refused to go escaped with Apache leaders Geronimo and Juh for a life on the run in the mountains of northern Mexico. Over the next ten years, the U.S. Army tracked and captured Geronimo, and returned him to the reservation where he would once again escape. In 1886, Geronimo and his band of 18 warriors and their families agreed to surrender to General Nelson Miles and his army of 5,000 soldiers. This represented the end of Indian resistance. The government sent Geronimo and his band to Florida prisons along with members who had settled on the San Carlos Reservation years earlier. Many prisoners died. The government sent the band's children to Indian boarding schools. The government later moved Geronimo to an Oklahoma reservation near Fort Sill and banned him from ever returning to his homelands in Arizona. Geronimo remains a hero, and his deep responsibility to protect his people has become legendary.

1858	1876-1886	1886	1904
Mexican army attacks Geronimo's camp and kills many, including Geronimo's wife, children, and mother	Repeatedly flees San Carlos Reservation with followers	Surrenders to United States Army and sent to prison	Appears at St. Louis World's Fair, selling autographs and souvenirs

Ghent, Treaty of signed in Europe on December 24, 1814, ended the War of 1812 fought between the United States and Great Britain. The war did not produce a clear winner, and both sides wanted peace. The two countries agreed to release all prisoners and give back to each other lands taken during the war. The news of the treaty did not reach America for several weeks. General Andrew Jackson in the meantime, was able to defeat the British in the battle for New Orleans on January 8, 1815. Fighting ended with news of the treaty, but the last battle helped Andrew Jackson later win the presidency of the United States.

Ghost Dance, practiced as part of the Ghost Dance movement especially among Plains peoples in the late 1800s, first surfaced in 1869 in today's Nevada. A Northern Paiute named Wodziwob had a dream about the future. In his dream, the Supreme Ruler came to the people along with the spirits of their dead. They would renew the land, life would never end, and all people would live in peace. Wodziwob taught his people the dance that went along with the ritual, a type of traditional round dance. Over time, the ritual died out. The Ghost Dance was brought back in the 1880s. This time, the movement spread rapidly, promising a return to old ways and the disappearance of nonnatives. It required tribes to give up alcohol, live in harmony with each other, and turn away

from the ways of nonnatives. The Lakota added the idea of Ghost Dance shirts. The Bureau of Indian Affairs banned the Ghost Dance, fearing a return of fighting and violence.

Ghost Dance shirts were sacred clothing worn by both Lakota men and women while performing the Ghost Dance ritual. The Lakota made the shirts from white muslin, a kind of plain, lightweight cotton cloth. The Lakota believed the shirts protected the wearer from bullets.

The Lakota decorated Ghost Dance shirts with fringe, symbols, and animal drawings.

WORDS TO KNOW

movement (MOOV-mihnt): a group of people with the same beliefs who are working together to accomplish certain goals

ritual (RIH-chew-uhl): a ceremony with a certain set of steps to perform in a certain order

Giago, Tim (1934-), a member of the Oglala Lakota tribe in South Dakota, founded the *Lakota Times* in 1981 on the Pine Ridge Reservation. Many nonnative people opposed him, often using death threats. Educated in business and journalism, he built several successful weekly newspapers and trained other Native American journalists and editors, who later started their own newspapers. He also created the Native American Journalists Association in 1984. In 2006, he wrote *Children Left Behind: The Dark Legacy of Indian Mission Boarding Schools.*

Gibbon, John (1827-1896) commanded the foot soldiers in the military operation to force Lakota chief Sitting Bull and his people onto reservation land. He coordinated an attack with George Armstrong Custer's cavalry unit, but Custer moved ahead too quickly. Gibbon arrived at the Battle of Little

Bighorn too late to save Custer and his men. He conducted a surprise attack on the Nez Perce at the Big Hole River as the Nez Perce fled across Montana to Canada under the leadership of Chief Joseph. Though the army lost the battle, it contributed to the eventual capture of the Nez Perce. He later commanded the U.S. Army in the Pacific Northwest.

Girty, Simon (1741-1818) acted as a liaison and interpreter between the British and the Native Americans who sided with them during the American Revolution. When Girty and his brothers were children, the Seneca kidnapped them during the Seven Years' War. During his years in captivity, he came to understand and prefer their way of life. During the American Revolution, he aided the colonial rebels, became dissatisfied, and then changed his loyalties to the British. Reportedly, he also refused to help Colonel William Crawford. He stood by as Crawford was tortured to death by the Delaware. Therefore, history often describes Girty as a villain and traitor. Other stories say that he saved the lives of many nonnative captives of the tribes over the years by defending them and sometimes paying for their freedom with his own money.

WORDS TO KNOW

cavalry (KAV-uhl-ree): soldiers on horseback

converts (KAHN-verts): people who have changed religions or beliefs

ethnic (ETH-nihk): relating to a particular culture or people

journalist (JER-nuh-lihst): someone who writes or reports news stories for a newspaper or magazine

liaison (lee-AY-zahn): someone who helps two groups communicate or cooperate

Giveaway Ceremony is a formal time for members of a tribe to share personal possessions with other tribal members, and in doing so, creating or cementing beneficial relationships or proving a tribe member's wealth. Sometimes the giver presents a gift to someone more powerful, or to someone able to do the giver a favor. Prized possessions given in the name of an ancestor honors them as well. Native peoples believe blessings will come to those participating in the ceremony. For traditionally nomadic people, giving things away kept personal possessions to a minimum for ease of travel, while making life easier for another tribe member.

Glancy, Diane (1941-), of Cherokee and European heritage, is an award-winning writer, poet, and educator. After receiving her Master of Fine Arts degree from the University of Iowa, she began teaching at Macalester College in Minnesota, where she was a Professor of English. Her writing has received the American Book Award, the Minnesota Book Award in Poetry, and many other prizes. She often writes about Native American life and tradition, how it fits in the modern world, and her own mixed heritage.

Gluskap (also known as Gluskabi or Glooscap) is a hero in the mythology of the Northeast native peoples. Gluskap and Malsum were sons of the great Earth Mother. Gluskap appears in the creation story as the maker of all things good, including the plains, plants, animals, and humans. His brother, the evil Malsum, began creating hazards like rocks, mountains, and snakes. After Malsum attempts to kill him, Gluskap saves the goodness he has created by killing Malsum. Gluskap lives on in other stories, too.

Gnadenhutten Massacre occurred in March 1782 at the Moravian Church mission in today's Gnadenhutten, Ohio. Pennsylvania militiamen led by Lieutenant Colonel David Williamson killed 96 Christian Delaware, including 28 men, 29 women, and 39 children. The militiamen wrongly accused the Native American converts of the murders of several Pennsylvania settlers. Though the massacre caused much protest, no trial occurred.

A 37-foot (11-meter) monument stands next to a reconstructed cabin in what was the center of the original village. The inscription reads: "Here triumphed in death ninety Christian Indians, March 8, 1782."

Gold seekers swirled and sifted gold from streams and riverbeds using a technique called panning.

Gold rush refers to the massive flocking of newcomers to an area where miners discover gold. Often the gold seekers did not have rights to the land where they wanted to hunt for gold. The Native Americans did. The lure of wealth caused an outcry for native lands whenever gold seekers made a new discovery. The discovery of gold prompted the United States government to repeatedly break treaties and push Native Americans off land to allow nonnative ownership. Gold seekers and others demanded Cherokee land in Georgia upon the discovery of gold in 1827. This led to the 1838 Trail of Tears, the forced removal of the Cherokee to western lands. California's gold rush brought miners and settlers, and along with them, diseases the native peoples had never seen. Smallpox, cholera, measles, and scarlet fever swept through the tribes, causing widespread death. Settlers claimed the best farmland, miners dumped mine waste into fishing streams, and starving tribes became a source of cheap labor. The Colorado gold rush of 1858 resulted in the destruction of the Cheyenne way of life. In 1874, gold in South Dakota's Black Hills prompted the U.S. government to approach Lakota Sioux leader Sitting Bull to ask for its sale. He refused to sell and the army attacked. Several years of fighting later, Congress passed a law taking the Black Hills land. The Klondike gold rush displaced the Han people in eastern Alaska and western Yukon Territory and left them in poverty.

See also: Trail of Tears

 WORDS TO KNOW

cholera (KAHL-er-uh): a contagious disease causing severe vomiting and diarrhea, often resulting in death

displaced (dihs-PLAYST): took the place of

influenced (ihn-FLEW-uhnsd): affected someone or something

scarlet fever (SKAR-liht FEE-ver): a contagious disease characterized by a high fever, a red, itchy rash all over the body, and sore throat; today antibiotics cure this illness

Where miners found gold, whole towns developed.

Goose, Mary (1955 -) helped start and lead the Native American Producers Alliance (NAPA) in 1993. NAPA champions the truth of Native American history and culture as told in film and television productions. Involvement in important productions and working behind the camera allows Native Americans to tell their story from their own point of view.

Gordon, Roxy (1945-2000) was a singer, songwriter, artist, and author of Choctaw and Assiniboine heritage. He lived in East Dallas, Texas, and operated a publishing company, Wowapi, with his wife, Judy. His writings provide an understanding of what it means to be Native American. He often illustrated his books with his own black and white drawings.

Tribes often made gorgets from shell or copper.

Gorget was originally a piece of metal armor designed to protect the throat in battle. European soldiers used gorgets and brought the tradition with them to the New World. Later, officers wore small ornamental gorgets on a neck chain to show their rank or authority. Some tribes wore a similar decoration as well, such as the Timucua of Florida.

Gorman, Rudolph Carl (1931-2005), a Navajo artist born on the reservation in Chinle, Arizona, created hundreds of paintings, ceramics, and sculptures showing traditional Native American women in common life moments as a way to honor them and show their timeless beauty. His father sculpted and painted artworks as well. Gorman spent time in Mexico with other gifted artists, including Diego Rivera, who influenced his work. The Metropolitan Museum of Art in New York presented a show featuring his work. The New York Times titled him, "The Picasso of American Indian Art."

Gould, Janice (1949-), a writer and poet of Maidu heritage, earned a Ph.D. in English from the University of New Mexico in 1995. She received a grant from the National Endowment for the Arts and served as the Hallie Ford Chair in Creative Writing for three years at Willamette University. She has taught Creative Writing, Women's Studies, and American Studies at the college level. She has written several books of poetry, including *Beneath My Heart* and *Earthquake Weather.*

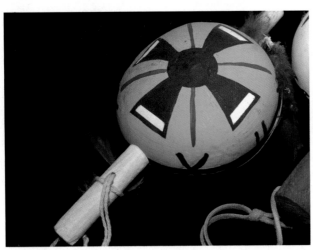

This painted Hopi gourd rattle accompanied seasonal ceremonies.

Gourd Dance originally honored victory in battle as part of a four-day festival. Kiowa, Comanche, Ute, and other tribes use this dance. The dancers move slowly to the song of a drum. Each dancer carries a gourd rattle, though modern dancers may choose a metal rattle. The dance purifies the dancing grounds before a powwow begins. Sometimes a gourd dance event stands alone, without a powwow. Kiowa legend says a red wolf gave the gourd dance and its songs to a lost warrior who shared them with his people. The howl at the end of the dance honors the red wolf. Men perform the gourd dance in the central circle; women may participate on the sidelines.

See also: powwow

Gourds, a fruit in the squash family, come in many shapes and colors. When dried, they become hollow.

Gourds proved to be useful to many tribes. They often fashioned musical instruments from gourds. Native Americans, particularly those in the Southwest and California, constructed ceremonial rattles from dried gourds, seeds, and wood handles. Cherokees carved gourd masks to use in storytelling. Many also carved gourd shells into dippers or curved spoons for cooking. Larger gourds served as water containers. Healers used their seeds as medicines.

Government rations, supplied to Native Americans on reservations by the United States, added to the humiliation of reservation life. Unable to support themselves as they once did, tribe members had to accept food rations which were often spoiled, in short supply, or late in arriving, but necessary to survival.

Governments varied among tribes. Commonly, a peace chief, a war chief and a healer, or shaman, guided a tribe. The shaman chiefdom passed from father to son, while the tribe usually appointed the peace and war chiefs. The peace chief negotiated agreements with other tribes and governments. The war chief led warriors in battle. The shaman provided wellness, healing, and blessings. He led ceremonies and handled other spiritual responsibilities. In some tribes, a clan leader, called a clan mother or clan father, headed extended family groups. Clans upheld cultural rules like division of work or selection of a spouse. Clan leaders chose council chiefs called sachems. Sachems, like those in the Iroquois League, worked to keep peace and looked out for the welfare of all people. Other tribes, like the Havasupai, had a single chief or headman.

Today the U.S. officially recognizes over 560 tribal governments. These governments may collect taxes, enforce laws, decide membership, and grant licenses. Tribes, like states, may not print money, declare war, or make agreements with foreign governments.

Metacomet, grand sachem of the Wampanoags, stands at a treaty table.

Gradual Civilization Act passed in Canada in 1857, required any Aboriginal male over the age of 21, able to speak, read, and write English or French, and who was free of debt, to give up his tribal identity and rights and become a British citizen. His wife and children would automatically become citizens as well, giving up their cultural heritage. For this, he would receive 50 acres (20 hectares) of land from the tribal holdings and money equal to his share of the tribal wealth. The act outraged Aboriginal peoples, for it undermined their tradition of community and forced their assimilation into the British way of life. Relations between the government and the natives broke down rapidly.

Grand Settlement of 1701

consisted of two separate treaties negotiated by the Five Nations of the Iroquois Confederacy. The first treaty with the French, and the other treaty with the British, settled the conflicts with the Europeans. The French and British were unaware of the terms of the other country's treaty. The French agreed to allow the Iroquois tribes to hunt and trade in the area known as New France, in exchange for staying out of conflicts between the French and British. The British received all the land the Iroquois tribes had gained in the Beaver War in their treaty.

Ulysses S. Grant, a military hero, had a troubled presidency.

Grant, Ulysses S. (1822-1885)

served as the 18th president of the United States, from 1869 to 1877. His winning military strategy as the top Civil War general in the Union Army gained him wide popularity in the North. His lack of experience in politics and government led to appointments of friends and wealthy men to positions of power, instead of reliable, experienced people he could trust to help him. His appointees, through carelessness, dishonesty, or lack of knowledge, caused scandals during his two terms in office. After his presidency and a world tour, he lost his money in bad investments and became seriously ill with cancer. He wrote his memoir while dying, in the hopes that book sales would support his family after his death. The memoir sold well and remains an important reference.

WORDS TO KNOW

politics (PAH-lih-tiks): activities related to governing a country or area

scandals (SKAN-duhlz): shocking behavior or wrongdoings

strategy (STRAT-uh-jee): an action plan

Grant's Peace Policy of 1869

recognized Native Americans as individual dependents of the federal government rather than as tribal groups, for their protection. A public outcry caused

President Grant to present this fix to the mistreatment of Native Americans and the wrongdoing on reservations by the Bureau of Indian Affairs. Grant appointed churchmen as agents in the Bureau and banned the unrequested use of military force on reservations. The policy failed. It did not stop native peoples from leaving the reservation or nonnative use of reservation lands.

Grass house is a type of dwelling built by the Wichita in the prairie region. The house resembled a haystack in shape, with a frame of long poles in a circle. The poles met together at the top to form a dome. Builders fastened the poles with bendable branches or tough reeds. They used thatch to cover the structure.

See also: Wichita

Inside a grass house, the pole framing and support beams show.

Grattan Defeat occurred in today's Wyoming near Fort Laramie in 1854. U.S. Army Lieutenant John L. Grattan and his men went to a Lakota camp to find the person accused of stealing a cow from a passing wagon train. Grattan had little experience in handling peaceful talks with Native Americans. The soldiers killed tribal leader Conquering Bear. The Lakota responded by killing Grattan and all his soldiers. This started a long chain of retaliation involving the Cheyenne and Lakota, called the Sioux Wars.

The Wichita covered their grass houses with tight bundles of grass, or thatch.

WORDS TO KNOW

retaliation (ree-tal-ee-AY-shun): revenge; repaying an attack with a similar attack

This map shows the Great Basin Culture Area.

Great Basin Culture Area

includes Utah, Nevada, and parts of Oregon, Idaho, Wyoming, Arizona, and Colorado. The Bannock, Paiute, Shoshone, and Ute tribes occupy this large, dry land. The area borders on desert, receiving only about 10 inches (25 cm) of precipitation each year. The Great Basin experiences hot summers and cold winters. Flanked on the west by the Sierra Nevada Mountains, and on the east by the Rocky Mountains, rivers here flow inward, not to the ocean. The harsh climate limits farming. Short grasses and sagebrush hold down the soil. In the hills, evergreen trees like juniper and piñon grow. Animals adapted to the dry climate live here, including pronghorn antelope, mountain goats, jackrabbits, rodents, snakes, lizards, and grasshoppers. The area includes the Great Salt Lake region.

See also: map on page 54

Great Basin Indians lived in the Great Basin Culture Area. They included the Bannock, Paiute, Shoshone, and Ute. Although many tribes have been shuffled around over time, some, like the Paiute and Washoe, still do live in the Great Basin Culture Area. All these tribes shared a similar lifestyle and, except for the Washoe, spoke Uto-Aztecan languages. The dry climate severely limited farming. Instead, they lived in small family groups, moving frequently to follow food sources.

The Eastern Shoshone used skin tepees that they could take with them when they moved.

The California gold rush and the discovery of silver in Nevada resulted in large numbers of newcomers passing through, and settling their territory. Trappers, traders, and mountain men roamed the area. In 1847, a religious group called the Mormons settled on the Great Salt Lake. They brought hogs, cattle, and other grazing animals. These domestic animals destroyed or ate the plants the tribes depended on for food, like the camas plant.

FACT FILE

Location: They lived in the Great Basin Culture Area including Utah, Nevada, and parts of Oregon, Idaho, Wyoming, and Colorado.

Housing: Most of the tribes built temporary pole frame homes covered with grass mats or brush that they could put together and take down quickly and easily.

Diet: They hunted antelope and jackrabbits and gathered berries, seeds, pine nuts, roots, insects, and grubs. Northern and eastern peoples also hunted bison and fished the rivers.

Interesting Fact: Because they dug for edible roots and grubs, the Great Basin peoples are sometimes called Digger Indians. Juicy roots provided an excellent source of water.

Before pioneers arrived in the area
- The Bannock and Northern Shoshone lived north of the Great Salt Lake into today's Idaho.
- The Eastern Shoshone lived east of them in today's Wyoming.
- The Ute occupied an area including parts of Colorado and Utah.
- The Southern Paiute roamed the southern part of today's Utah and northern Arizona.
- The Western Shoshone lived in today's Nevada.
- The Northern Paiute lived in southeastern Oregon area.

Minor tribes including the Washoe, Mono, Panamint Shoshone, Kawaiisu, and Chemehuevi lived in pockets on the western edge of the Great Basin.

The shaded area defines the Great Plains Culture Area.

Great Plains Culture Area refers to the vast grasslands in central North America between the Mississippi River in the east and the Rocky Mountains in the west. It stretches from Canada all the way to the Rio Grande River in Texas. Huge bison herds thrived on the grasses along with caribou, antelope, and game birds. Predators like eagles and wolves hunted the grass eaters. In the north, cold, snowy winters followed hot, windy summers. The land shaped the culture of the people who lived there. Many tribes made their homes there and shared similar cultures.

See also: map on page 54

Great Plains Indians once lived across central North America. This windswept, treeless grassland supported dozens of tribes. For many plains tribes, life centered on bison hunting. Prior to the arrival of Europeans, indigenous peoples hunted on foot with bows and arrows. Tribes followed the herds and lived a nomadic lifestyle. Dogs worked beside them, carrying and pulling loads. The Spaniards brought horses, and as tribes acquired them, hunts became more efficient. Hunting became even easier with the arrival of guns. Tribes traded furs for guns, horses, metals, and other European goods.

Tribes living near riverbanks supported themselves with farming, too. Women planted crops, tended the fields, and harvested the food. Tribes commonly held ceremonies and dances themed around the growing season.

Before nonnatives took over the land
- The Dakota, Lakota, and Nakota, together called Sioux by the French, lived in the north.
- The Gros Ventre, Blackfeet, Assiniboine, and Crow neighbors lived to their west.
- The Hidatsa, Arikara, and Mandan moved around together, to avoid war with the Dakota and Lakota Sioux and clashes with nonnatives, settling in the northern plains.
- Southern plains peoples, such as the Comanche, Kiowa, and Caddo, lived in today's Texas and southern Oklahoma.
- Central plains tribes included Arapaho, Cheyenne, Kaw, Missouria, Omaha, Osage, Otoe, Pawnee, Ponca, Quapaw, Tonkawa, and Wichita.

FACT FILE

Location: The broad sweep of grasslands covers the central United States and south-central Canada.

Diet: They hunted bison, antelope, and other game, grew crops such as corn, tobacco, beans, and gourds or pumpkins, and gathered wild plant foods.

Housing: Nomadic peoples preferred tepees or other temporary housing while those who stayed in one place or returned to a place year after year built earth lodges.

Sioux peoples sewed buckskin clothing like this colorful, fringed dress.

Interesting Fact: Plains peoples actively managed the land for native plants and animals. They set the grasses afire every few years to remove the old, dead grasses and tree seedlings and release the nutrients held in them back into the soil for new growth.

Great Spirit refers to native peoples' one Supreme Being, or god. They believe the Great Spirit created the universe and dwells in living things and places. The Great Spirit speaks through dreams and hears prayers. The Lakota call the Great Spirit *Wakan Tanka* while Algonquians speak of *Gitchi Manitou*.

Great Swamp Fight, the decisive battle in King Philip's War, occurred in today's Rhode Island in December 1675. The Wampanoag, Nipmuc, and Narragansett, led by Metacomet, joined to push colonists from tribal lands during the summer and fall of 1675. Plymouth governor Josiah Winslow's forces attacked and burned a large Narragansett village, killing about a third of the tribe. Afterward, resistance from area tribes stopped.

Green Corn Ceremony brought renewal and forgiveness and prepared Southeast tribes like the Creek, Seminole, and Cherokee for the new year. Villagers repaired and cleaned their homes. Some fasted. A corn feast, the lighting of a Sacred Fire, and the Green Corn Dance followed. A feast, games, more dancing, and a purifying bath completed the ceremony.

Greene, Graham (1952-), an Oneida born in Ontario, Canada, has appeared in many television and film roles. He played the role of Kicking Bird in the 1990 film, *Dances with Wolves*, for which he received an Academy Award nomination. Canada honored him with the Earle Grey Award for Lifetime Achievement at the 2004 Gemini Awards.

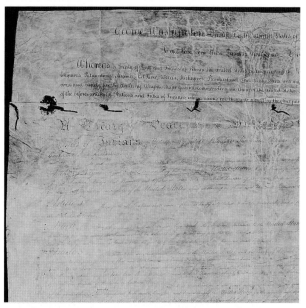

The National Archives in Washington, D.C., has the original Treaty of Greenville.

Greenville, Treaty of was signed by leaders from many tribes including the Shawnee, Miami, Potawatomi, and Delaware on August 20, 1795, following their defeat at the Battle of Fallen Timbers in 1794. In the agreement, the tribes gave up most of Ohio to the United States and moved west. The Shawnee, Tecumseh, refused to sign, and later united tribes in a renewed resistance movement against the United States.

Edward S. Curtis photographed these Gros Ventre warriors in 1908.

Gros Ventre (also called the A'ani or A'aninin, meaning *white clay people*) lived on the plains of northern Montana and southern Canada between the Missouri and Saskatchewan Rivers. They encountered early French fur traders there who called them Gros Ventre, or big belly. In the tribe's sign language, the sign for their tribe was a full sweeping motion over the stomach. Their neighbors and former allies, the Blackfeet, named them the Atsina. The Gros Ventre believed the Creator made them from clay as his companions. The Cree, after getting guns from fur traders, pushed the Gros Ventre south out of Canada. As Plains people, they depended largely on bison for food. They also farmed during the brief summers. They sheltered in large tepees. Like many other Native American tribes, diseases from the incoming traders and pioneers reduced their numbers greatly. By 1888, less than 600 members remained.

Facing an uncertain future, they agreed to sell their land to gold miners and moved to the Fort Belknap Reservation, which they share with the Assiniboine.

Guadalupe Hidalgo, Treaty of

ended the Mexican-American War on February 2, 1848. The war sought to end the border argument between Mexico and the United States. Treaty talks began in August 1847. The treaty stated that Mexico would turn over more than half its lands, including today's Arizona, California, New Mexico, and parts of Colorado, to the United States in exchange for war damage repayment totaling $15 million. The treaty also set the border between the two countries at the Rio Grande River and promised to protect and honor the property of the Mexican people who would be living within the United States' new border.

Guns changed the way the tribes hunted for food and the way the tribes related to each other. French and British traders first introduced guns to native peoples in the 1600s. Native peoples continued to hunt with bows and arrows, especially in the early days of gun use. The early guns handled awkwardly and needed gunpowder and shot that could only be gotten from traders. With improved guns and horses, however, Plains Indians had much better success on bison hunts. As meat replaced agriculture, native peoples moved around more, following the herds. In warfare, too, the tribes eventually preferred guns, though they still used bows and arrows and war clubs, too. Armed tribes gained land by forcing neighboring tribes without guns to leave.

Haida made sea journeys in huge boats carved from the massive trunks of red cedar trees. These boats could hold up to 60 warriors.

Weavers made clothing and containers using the long, tough strands of cedar tree bark. Animal furs provided warm clothing. Haida society consisted of two clans, the Eagle and the Raven. Shamans provided spiritual leadership.

After fur traders arrived, smallpox and other diseases killed many Haida. Liquor and missionary teachings further eroded their culture. The Haida won a battle in the Supreme Court in Canada in 2004 giving them additional control over timber sales on their lands. A national marine conservation area is being established on part of the islands to further protect the land. The Haida have also worked to change the name of the Queen Charlotte Islands, so named by a British fur trader in 1787, back to the original Haida Gwaii, meaning *Islands of the People*.

FACT FILE

Language: The Haida speak a Na-Dene language.

Location: They live on the Queen Charlotte Islands off the coast of British Columbia, Canada, and Prince of Wales Island, Alaska.

Diet: The Haida hunted, fished, and gathered to meet their food needs. They smoked the fish they caught to preserve it through the winter. Coastal native peoples, including the Haida, harvested candlefish from streams during the spring. When boiled, these small, fatty fish released rich oil used for cooking and lamps.

Housing: They built large homes made of wooden planks and gables holding several families. Houses stretched up to 6,000 square feet (557 square meters) in size, or more if it was a chief's house. The Haida build modern houses today, though may still use traditional house decorations and totem poles.

Interesting Fact: Haida carved masks, totem poles, chests, headdresses, warriors' shields and children's toys.

See also: Haida legend page 56

A Haida totem pole stands at Thunderbird Park in Victoria, British Columbia.

Hale, Janet Campbell (1947-), a
Native American author, grew up on the
Yakima reservation in Washington and the
Coeur d'Alene reservation in Idaho. During
an unhappy childhood, she found escape
through writing. At 23 she wrote her first
book, *The Owl's Song*. She went on to
graduate from the University of California
and continued her education by attending
law school and completing an advanced
degree in English. She won the American
Book Award in 1994 for *Bloodlines:
Odyssey of a Native Daughter*. She often
writes about women's courage, racism,
mixed blood, self-respect, and pride
in heritage.

Hall, Louis Karoniaktajeh (1918-
1993) was a Mohawk writer, artist, and
spokesperson born in Quebec, Canada.
He believed in armed self-defense of the
First Peoples' right to govern, or
sovereignty. He promoted rebuilding the
Iroquois Confederacy with a religion of
peace, but with guns as support. He
served as a chief for 19 years. He wrote
and distributed newsletters promoting
his ideas.

WORDS TO KNOW

league (LEEG): a group of people that join together for
a certain purpose or desire to cooperate; a confederacy

spokesperson (SPOHKS-per-sun): someone who tells of
the desires, beliefs, or interests of a group of people on
their behalf

Hallalhotsoot, Chief (about 1795-
1876) was the son of Twisted Hair, the Nez
Perce man who aided the Lewis and Clark
expedition in 1805. His talkative nature
and ability to speak English earned him
the nickname Lawyer, by area nonnatives.
He believed that befriending the
nonnatives, as his father had, was the way
to a peaceful and better future. The tribe
selected him as their main spokesperson in
treaty negotiations with the United States
at the Walla Walla Treaty Council of 1855.

*Students studied agriculture at the
Hampton Institute.*

Hampton Institute, one of the first
colleges for African Americans, opened its
doors in Virginia in 1868. Former Civil
War Union Brigadier General Samuel
Chapman Armstrong founded the school.
Ten years later, it began accepting Native
American students as part of the
assimilation movement. Many nonnatives
at that time believed the best way to solve
conflicts with native peoples was to force

them to leave behind native ways and learn the culture of those of European heritage. The Hampton Institute promoted the concept of learning by doing, and taught the practical skills of farming, business, housekeeping, sewing, building, and learning to read, write, and speak English. Many students, taken forcibly from their families in order to attend the school, lived there as well.

See also: Indian boarding schools

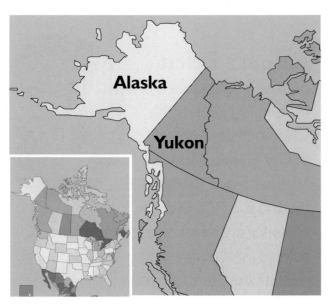

Han (meaning *people of the river*) people lived in eastern Alaska and western Yukon Territory. A woodland people, the Han fished and hunted moose and caribou. In summer, the forest produced berries and the rivers supplied them with salmon and pike. They constructed lodges out of poles set in a tent shape with covers of animal skins, moss, or bark. The Han traveled by birch bark or moose hide canoes, snowshoes, and sleds. They also used animal skins to make clothing. A large Han

village flourished at the meeting point of the Yukon and Klondike Rivers, where prospectors struck gold in 1896. Just two years later, more than 30,000 newcomers had invaded the Han homelands, hunting and taking timber along with the gold. The 1990s brought the Comprehensive Land Claim Agreement between Canada's government and the Han. This agreement intends to settle disagreements about land and resource rights on tribal lands and offers a measure of fairness and opportunity for the Han.

Handsome Lake (1735-1815) a Seneca in the Iroquois League during a time of poverty and hopelessness, had a vision in 1799. He dreamed that the Creator showed him instructions for a new way of life for the peoples in the confederacy. Handsome Lake made it his goal to teach them this new way, which combined old ways with Christian ideas. He taught a message of peace, the importance of farming and education, the rejection of alcohol, and the halt of land sales to the United States. The new way, sometimes called the Code of Handsome Lake, included traditional ceremonies and festivals, too. Iroquois life and values today still reflect Handsome Lake's spiritual path.

WORDS TO KNOW

pike (PIKE): a freshwater fish that can be found throughout the northern hemisphere

Great Bear Lake lies in Canada's Northwest Territories.

Hare

(also known as Kawchottine or Kawchodinne, meaning *people of the great hares*) tribe lived around and near Great Bear Lake and the Mackenzie River in Canada's far northern Mackenzie Territory, in the Subarctic Culture Area. A forest and tundra people, they hunted caribou, musk ox, beaver, muskrat, ptarmigan, and Arctic hares for food and clothing. They fished in the rivers and gathered berries. To their north lived the Inuit, their enemies. They mostly avoided warring with other tribes. The Hare spoke an Athabaskan language. Alexander Mackenzie, a fur trader and explorer, arrived at what was later named the Mackenzie River in 1789. The Northwest Company built Fort Good Hope and Fort Norman in Hare country in the early 1800s. The population, estimated at 750 in 1670, dropped to 467 by 1878. Today Hare descendants number about 1,000.

See also: Subarctic Culture Area

Harjo, Joy

(1951-) writes poetry, stories, and songs that reflect her Muscogee Creek heritage. One of her stories, *The Good Luck Cat*, a children's picture book, provides a look at Native American identity and culture. Her books of poetry have received the Oklahoma Book Arts Award and an American Book Award. She received the American Indian Distinguished Achievement in the Arts Award, too. Her band, *Poetic Justice,* set her poetry to music.

Harmar's Defeat

occurred over three days in October 1790, when military forces led by General Josiah Harmar failed to conquer the tribes in the Old Northwest. Harmar's men included 320 soldiers and over 1,000 mostly untrained militiamen. Harmar ordered two attacks, but Miami war chief Little Turtle with the Shawnee Blue Jacket and their warriors, won easily each time. His loss resulted in more attacks on area settlers by native peoples.

See also: Little Turtle's War and Miami

Harmony Ethic, Cherokee

embraces a spirit of cooperation and respect towards others. The Cherokee believe every life has value and purpose. Treating others with kindness and generosity creates unity and balance in the tribe and results in a healthy mind, body, and spirit for tribal members. In the past, nearly all tribes recognized the need for community and the important role social bonds played in survival. Many native peoples had a set of beliefs surrounding interaction with others that continues, at least in part, today.

A rope attached to the harpoon enables this hunter to pull in his catch.

Harney, William S. (1800-1889)

began his military career in 1818 as an officer in the U.S. Army. He fought in the Seminole, Blackhawk, Mexican-American, and Civil Wars. After the Grattan Defeat of 1854, Harney ordered an attack on a Brule Lakota camp at Blue Creek in today's Nebraska, believing them to be responsible for the attack on Grattan's forces. They killed 86 people and captured 70 women and children. He later served on the U.S. Peace Commission in negotiating the second Treaty of Fort Laramie with the Lakota.

See also: Grattan Defeat

Harpoon is a weapon used mainly in

hunting fish and sea animals like whales and seals. It has a sharp, pointed head attached to a long wooden pole. Most often, tribes who lived by the sea used harpoons, including the Timucua in Florida, and the Micmac, Kutchin, Algonquians, and Inuit in the north.

Harris, Ladonna (1931-) has voiced

strong support for Native Americans and acted on their behalf. Born in Oklahoma of Comanche and Irish-American heritage, Harris has provided leadership in the areas of housing opportunity, mental health, the environment, land resource rights, and telecommunications in the United States and the world. In 1970, she founded Americans for Indian Opportunity, which strives to strengthen tribal organizations and Native American community leaders. In the 1970s, she worked for the United Nations Education, Scientific, and Cultural Organization (UNESCO) and served as an advisor in the Office of Economic Opportunity.

WORDS TO KNOW

advisor (ad-VYE-zer): someone who provides opinions, information, and suggestions to decision makers

William H. Harrison won the nickname, Old Tip or Old Tippecanoe, for his success at the Battle of Tippecanoe.

Harrison, William Henry (1773-1841)

was the ninth president of the United States. In college, he first studied classics and history, then medicine. He left school to join the United States Army and served in the Battle of Fallen Timbers in today's Ohio, which opened the area to settlement. He later became Secretary of the Northwest Territory and Governor of the Indiana Territory. His responsibilities as governor included getting tribal lands for new settlements and defending those settlements from native peoples. In 1811 as part of the Indian Wars, he led 1,000 men in the defeat of Tecumseh's warriors at the Battle of Tippecanoe. In the War of 1812, as a brigadier general in the army, he defeated the British and native forces in the Battle of the Thames, fought in 1813. Tecumseh died during this battle. Following the war, the public praised Harrison as a military hero and elected him president. He died of pneumonia after only one month in office.

See also: Tecumseh

Hataali

is a Navajo word for a healer who used special knowledge and chants to mend physical and mental ills. A Hataali acted as a helper and guide for the patient through the healing process.

Hatuey

(unknown-1512) was a chief of the Taíno, or Arawak, on the island of Hispaniola, which lies between Cuba and Puerto Rico. Spanish explorer Christopher Columbus brought over 1,000 colonists to Hispaniola in 1493 to begin the first lasting colony in the New World. The Spanish demanded payment from the Taíno in gold or crops. If they could not pay, the Spanish forced them to work in their fields and mines. The Spanish also brought deadly diseases to the island. In the early 1500s, Hatuey fought against the Spanish. Spanish conqueror Diego Velásquez staged an attack on Cuba from Hispaniola in 1511. Hatuey and 400 Taíno reached Cuba first to warn the people. They did not believe him and the Spanish conquered Cuba. Hatuey led the Taíno in limiting Spanish settlement on Hispaniola until his capture by the Spanish and punishment by death.

See also: Hispaniola

several Pacific military operations including the Battle of Iwo Jima, where he and five other servicemen were photographed raising the American flag during the battle. The photograph brought him fame. He received the Commendation Ribbon with V combat device for heroic achievement. The V stands for valor. His unit also received the Presidential Unit Citation with one star for its service in Iwo Jima.

Havasu Falls spills 100 feet (30 meters) into a turquoise pool.

Havasupai (meaning *people of the blue water*) live in Havasu Canyon, a far removed part of the Grand Canyon of the Colorado River in Arizona. The Havasupai, descended from the Yuma people, speak a form of Yuman language. They farm the valley and irrigate their crops with water from the river. They also hunt up on the plateau above the canyon. The Havasupai have lived in the area for over 800 years. Talented weavers create baskets using local willow and cottonwood trees. Visitors seek the area to see the Havasu waterfalls. Tourism is their main source of income.

Felix de Weldon used the famous photograph of Hayes and his fellow Marines to sculpt the USMC War Memorial, located next to Arlington National Cemetery near Washington, D.C.

Hayes, Ira Hamilton (1923-1955), a Pima from the Gila River Reservation in Arizona, joined the United States Marine Corps during World War II. He served in

WORDS TO KNOW

classics (KLAS-ihks): a school subject where students study ancient Greek and Latin writings, ideas, and history

irrigate (EAR-uh-gayt): to bring water to crops, usually by digging a channel or waterway between a water source and the crops

plateau (pla-TOH): an area of high, mostly flat ground; a mesa

valor (VAL-er): extraordinary courage and daring in the face of danger

Captain Jack Hays and his Texas Rangers changed frontier fighting with their use of Colt revolvers.

Hays, John C. (1817-1883)

nicknamed Jack, was born in Tennessee and moved to the Republic of Texas at age 19, where he joined the Texas Rangers, a rough-and-ready branch of the Texan army. By 1840, his achievements and natural leadership abilities in the fight against Mexico had gained him the rank of captain. He continued to lead the Rangers during the Mexican-American War and fought alongside and against different native tribes. During his years in Texas, he tried to learn as much as he could about Native American war methods. This knowledge aided him in battle and made him skilled in warfare against Texas Native Americans. He rose in rank to colonel. After the war, he moved to California. He founded the city of Oakland and became involved with government, ranching, and real estate.

Hazen, William B. (1830-1887)

born in Vermont, graduated from the United States Military Academy at West Point in 1855. From there the army sent him west to fight in tribal wars in Texas, New Mexico, and Oregon. In six years of fighting, he earned the rank of captain for leadership and bravery. In 1861, he returned to West Point to teach battle methods to foot soldiers. When the Civil War started, he led soldiers in the Battles of Nashville, Shiloh, Perrysville, and Stone's River. After the Civil War, William B. Hazen served in the West, where he had run-ins with George Custer and their commanding officer, General Philip Sheridan, over how Native Americans should be treated. Sheridan and Custer labeled all native tribes as the enemy, while Hazen desired to judge each band on its behavior.

Headdresses

are Native American head coverings or bands made and decorated in particular ways and worn by special people for important events or ceremonies. Headdresses reflect the tribe's culture, and hold unique meaning to the person wearing it. Feathers hold special meaning to native peoples. They often attach feathers from birds important to the tribe or the ceremony to a band beaded with patterns or colors. The Plains peoples construct warbonnets from eagle feathers, cloth, leather, and beads. Only a very brave and important warrior who had

Proven Plains warriors wore warbonnets for ceremonies and important occasions.

proved himself in battle would earn the honor of wearing it. Many North American native peoples attach sacred meaning to eagles and their feathers. During his lifetime, a Lakota warrior earns one feather each time he shows bravery or endures

This Blackfoot cap features owl and red-tailed hawk feathers, split buffalo horn, and a beaded headband.

hardship on behalf of the tribe. Apache warriors wear soft leather caps decorated with bead designs and feathers. In one Hopi ceremony, women wear painted headdresses to ensure a successful harvest. Ancient Aztec royalty wore tall headdresses made from the bright green feathers of the quetzal, a bird sacred to them.

See also: feathers

This Blackfoot hat consists of bison fur and antelope horns.

Heathen is a negative word for a person who practices a religion that has many gods. It might also refer to someone who does not believe in Christianity, Judaism, the Muslim religion, or another widely held belief system with one supreme god. Many Europeans, colonists, and settlers looked down upon First Peoples as heathens.

WORDS TO KNOW

real estate (REEL es-TAYT): property that can be bought or sold

A 1740 portrait shows Hendrick in English clothing.

Meet Hendrick

Hendrick (about 1680-1755) (also known as Theyanoguin meaning *the western door is open*) served as a Mohawk chief, or sachem, and a leader of the Iroquois Confederacy. The confederacy had supported the British against the French since the mid-1600s. Hendrick continued to side with the British and worked to guard Mohawk rights and territory in colonial New York. He traveled with other native leaders to England to meet with Queen Anne and to ask for help against the French. Because of his work, he earned the nickname King Hendrick. He believed the British should form a confederacy as the natives had and live in peace. When British traders and frontiersmen began cheating the natives and seeking their land, he led missions of diplomacy to the British government in New York, warning them of the confederacy's fading support of the British. William Johnson persuaded Hendrick to join him and his men on a mission to raid the French's Fort St. Frederic. During the journey, the French and their allies surprised Johnson, Hendrick, and their men near Lake George. The attackers killed Hendrick and many others. This ended William Johnson's influence with the Mohawks.

About 1690	1711	1740	1754
Moved to Mohawk Valley, became Christian	Supported British in war against French	Second voyage to England; met King George II	Warned British of the Iroquois Confederacy's shift to support the French

Henry, Gordon, Jr. (1955-) a member of the White Earth band of Ojibwe of Minnesota, writes poetry and novels about Native American culture. His book, *The Light People*, received the 1995 American Book Award. He earned an advanced degree in literature at the University of North Dakota. He teaches classes in American literature, writing, and Native American literature at Michigan State University.

Henson, Lance David (1944-) of Cheyenne, Oglala Lakota, and French heritage, writes poetry and plays. He was raised in the Cheyenne tradition in Oklahoma. He served as a United States marine in the Vietnam War and received advanced education degrees from the Oklahoma College of Liberal Arts, now the University of Science and Arts of Oklahoma, and the University of Tulsa. Henson's many books of poetry have been translated into 25 languages around the world. Judges at the 1992 Oklahoma Book Awards selected two books of his poetry as finalists. In 2004, the University of Science and Arts of Oklahoma named Henson to the Alumni Hall of Fame.

Hertel, Francois (1642-1722) became
a military hero, interpreter, and frontiersman in French Canada. The Mohawks kidnapped him as a young man and adopted him into their tribe. During his two years with them, he learned how to battle like a Mohawk and sharpened his frontier skills. He later joined the French military. During King William's War in 1690, Hertel led French troops and their allies, the Abenakis, in a night raid against the British settlement of Salmon Falls in today's New Hampshire. Those they did not kill, they took as captives and marched north. The French government rewarded Hertel's military efforts and honored his family.

Heyoka (meaning *sacred clown*) plays
an important role in the Lakota culture. He acts in ridiculous or funny ways, much as a jester or trickster would. For example, if the people were suffering from heat, the heyoka would take their minds off it by pretending to be cold, shivering, and covering himself with a blanket. Heyokas show others wise choices by their seemingly foolish acts.

Hiawatha (born and died before the
arrival of settlers) (also known as Ayenwatha) served as an Onondaga and Mohawk chief. He believed in the ideas of the Great Peacemaker who gave him a vision of a great, united league of tribes living in peace. Each tribe of the league would have its own government, but one overall government would also guide the tribes. According to the vision, the league would eventually include all the tribes of man, so there would be lasting peace. Hiawatha's powerful words convinced five northeastern tribes to form the Five Nations of the Iroquois, including the Seneca, Onondaga, Mohawk, Oneida, and Cayuga peoples. In the early 1700s, the Tuscarora joined the confederacy and then it became the Six Nations.

Hickok, Wild Bill

(1837-1876), born James Butler Hickok, gained fame in the old Wild West. He drove a stagecoach, and then became a lawman and gunfighter in the territories of Kansas and Nebraska. He served as a scout, wagon master, courier, and spy in the Civil War for the North. For a short time, he served as a cavalryman under Custer in the Indian Wars. He died in Deadwood, Dakota Territory, while playing cards in a saloon.

Hidatsa (also known as Minitaree and Minitari) are Plains Indians living in today's North Dakota. The French called them the Gros Ventre of the River, but this is a separate tribe from the Gros Ventre of Montana. The Hidatsa lived in earth lodges. The entire community helped build the house. After construction, the family who would live in the house held a feast for the village. The Hidatsa women farmed large gardens. The men traded with Europeans, European-Americans, and other tribes for guns, liquor, beads, tools, cloth, and later, horses. When the Hidatsa got horses, they, like other Plains tribes, changed to a way of life centered on bison hunting. The bison provided food, shelter, and clothing. Smallpox swept through the region in 1781, and again in 1837, killing many. Afterward, the Hidatsa gathered together to form one village. In 1870, the United States government moved the Hidatsa, the Mandan, and the Arikara peoples, known as the Three Affiliated Tribes, to a reservation in North Dakota. In the 1950s when the Garrison Dam was built, one quarter of their reservation was flooded, including their best farmland, their hospital, many houses, and tribal headquarters. The United States government paid to relocate the homes then, but only in 2003 did it pay to replace the hospital. In 1993, the Three Affiliated Tribes opened a casino and lodge, which attracts visitors and brings a steady source of income into the reserve.

While traveling with a German explorer in the 1830s, Karl Bodmer recorded Native American cultures through his paintings, including this portrait of a Hidatsa chief.

Hieroglyphics, a form of writing, consist of hieroglyphs, or simple drawings of objects or shapes. Each hieroglyph symbolizes a word, part of a word, or sound. Some ancient peoples used hieroglyphs to record events, daily life, or stories. Most famously, the ancient Egyptians wrote this way, but ancient peoples in the New World also used this form of communication.

WORDS TO KNOW

casino (kuh-SEE-noh): a place to play games of chance for money, like card and dice games

courier (KOOR-ee-ur): someone who delivers goods or messages

obsidian (ahb-SIH-dee-uhn): a dark, hard stone used to make sharp blades or arrowheads

Mayan writings used hieroglyphs to represent time, events, things, words, and sounds.

Highway, Tomson (1951-), a
Canadian of Cree heritage, writes award-winning plays and books for both children and adults. He received Dora Mavor Moore Awards for his plays, *The Rez Sisters*, and *Dry Lips Oughta Move to Kapuskaking.* He often writes of reservation life and First Nations traditions and culture.

Hilbert, Vi (1918-), of Skagit heritage,
has made it her goal to preserve the language and culture of her people. She grew up in the Puget Sound area of Washington, in a home where family members spoke both English and Lushootseed. The legendary Chief Seattle also spoke Lushootseed. She learned not only to speak it, but as an adult learned to write it, too. Hilbert helped translate the recordings of elders speaking Lushootseed into English. She learned the stories passed down from the elders, and now that she is an elder herself, passes the stories down to the younger generations. She has published a dictionary in Lushootseed, and many collections of traditional stories.

Hispaniola is a mountainous island in the Caribbean Sea between Cuba and Puerto Rico. Native people called the island Quisqueya, meaning *mother of the earth.* Spanish explorer Christopher Columbus made two visits to Hispaniola, in 1492 and 1493. On the second visit, he established the first lasting colony in the New World. He brought 17 ships loaded with over 1,000 settlers, along with dogs, horses, pigs, cattle, sheep, goats, chickens, seeds, wheat, sugarcane, and cuttings to start peach and orange trees. These new animals and plants invaded the land as much as the colonists did. The domestic animals devoured native plants. The Spaniards enslaved the native people, the Taíno or Arawak, and treated them harshly. They also brought diseases. Smallpox, measles, the bubonic plague, influenza, and cholera swept through the islanders in terrible waves. In 1492, Hispaniola had an estimated population of nearly 8 million native people. Just 43 years later, in 1535, nearly all the Taíno had died, and with them their culture.

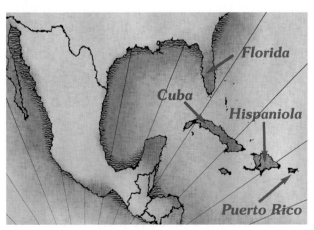

Today, two countries, Haiti and the Dominican Republic, share Hispaniola.

Hobson, Geary (1941-), of Cherokee-Quapaw and Chickasaw heritage, writes poetry and fiction and teaches Native American and American literature at the university level. He grew up in Arkansas and worked many different jobs, giving him a broad range of life experiences. He earned his living as a farm laborer, salesperson, construction worker, bookstore clerk, and semi-pro baseball player, and served in the United States marines. He received advanced degrees from Arizona State University and the University of New Mexico. His book, *The Last of the Ofos*, won him the 2001 Fiction Writer of the Year award from Wordcraft Circle of Native Writers and Storytellers. He received the Lifetime Achievement Award from the Native Writers' Circle of the Americas in 2003.

Hogan, from the Navajo word *hooghan* meaning *place home*, refers to a traditional Navajo shelter used for important ceremonies and times in the life of the family. In Navajo myth, Coyote, First Man, and First Woman appeared on land and, with instructions from the beavers, built the first hogan. The first hogan, a male hogan, is important in religious ceremonies and the Blessingway. The female hogan has a round shape. Dried mud fills the cracks in its log walls. The door to the hogan faces east to honor the sun. The female hogan offers families a place to pray, talk, entertain, and share stories. Although

almost no one lives in a hogan today, many people of Navajo descent feel incomplete without one and build a hogan next to their house. Modern hogans may have a refrigerator, sink, television, furniture, and a bathroom.

Female hogans bring a family together informally.

Hogan, Linda (1947-), a Chickasaw, has built a career as a writer, poet, and supporter of the environment. She earned an advanced degree from the University of Colorado in 1978. She writes about Native American identity, women, spirituality, and the human connection to nature. Her work has received many awards and honors, including being selected as a finalist for a Pulitzer Prize in Literature in 1990, the Lifetime Achievement Award by the Native Writers' Circle of the Americas in 1998, and Writer of the Year Wordcraft Circle Award in 2002.

Visitors to the Casa Grande Ruins National Monument in Arizona can see the remains of ancient Hohokam buildings.

Hohokam people, the ancestors of the Pima and possibly the Tohono O'odham, farmed in the Sonoran Desert of Arizona near the Gila River. Historians believe the Hohokam migrated north out of Mexico around 300 B.C. Between the years A.D. 800 to 1400, they built advanced water delivery systems to irrigate their crops. The networks of canals carried water hundreds of miles, allowing them dependable harvests of corn, beans, squash, and cotton. Nomadic no longer, they founded settlements including Snaketown, near today's Phoenix. A community of between 300 and 600 people existed there for about 1,200 years. The Hohokam traded turquoise, copper, and other goods with the Anasazi and the Mogollon. They valued shells and used them to make necklaces and religious objects. Other crafts included clay pottery decorated with red designs. Their Mesoamerican roots can be seen in their use of ball courts and decorative feathers. Archeologists received permission to excavate the ruins of Snaketown for a limited time in the 1930s and 1960s. After the last dig, they respected the wishes of the Gila River Indian Reservation where Snaketown is located and covered the ruins with soil once again.

Hole-in-the-Day, the Elder (about 1800-1847) and his brother, Strong Ground, belonged to the Mississippi Ojibwe tribe, also called Anishinaabe, located in today's Minnesota. Their tribe's chief, Curly Head, had no children and looked on the brothers as sons. Hole-in-the-Day and Strong Ground aided Curly Head in fighting their enemy, the Dakota Sioux, and in treaty negotiations with the United States government. When Curly Head died, the brothers led the Mississippi Ojibwe. Hole-in-the-Day believed the Mississippi Ojibwe should become like the area settlers in order to survive and he wanted to work for peace. Hole-in-the-Day died in 1845. His son, Kwi-wi-sens adopted his father's name, becoming Hole-in-the-Day, the Younger.

WORDS TO KNOW

Anishinaabe (ah-NIH-shih-nah-bay): the name that Ojibwe peoples call themselves

Pulitzer Prize (PULL-it-ser PRIZE): a well-known award for achievement in journalism, literature, and music writing, presented by the United States each year

spirituality (speer-ih-chew-AL-ih-tee): religious beliefs, or guiding beliefs about things that affect the spirit or soul of a person

Chief Hole-in-the-Day, the Younger, adopted the culture of the settlers in many ways, including his clothing, his home, and his acceptance of farming.

Hole-in-the-Day, the Younger

(1828-1868) (also known as Kwi-wi-sens as a child meaning *the boy*) was the son of the Mississippi Ojibwe chief Hole-in-the-Day, the Elder, who trained him to be a brave warrior and leader. Like his father, he spoke clearly and convincingly on behalf of the Mississippi Ojibwe, and continued his father's efforts to bring the culture of area settlers to the tribe.

Hole-in-the-Day handled business deals and treaties with government officials, including timber and land sales, boundary treaties between the Mississippi Ojibwe and Dakota Sioux, and peace treaties. He traveled six times to Washington, D.C., to meet with officials who had the power to defend the Mississippi Ojibwe when treaty promises were broken, or when new treaties were needed. He asked the government to grant native peoples citizenship. Hole-in-the-Day wished his people to be farmers, and not be dependent on government payments. He built a frame house, barn, and ferry crossing in order to lead his people by example. He continued to lead war parties as a method of justice.

Over his life, however, he made many enemies, both among those of European descent and native peoples. In 1868, Pillager tribesmen hired by local businessmen shot him to death.

Hollywood Indians and Indian Images

did not reflect the true history or cultures of real native peoples. Movies categorized them as either wise, noble people with many lessons to teach nonnatives, or savage warriors and heathens to be feared and killed. Neither of these images could possibly apply to all First Peoples. In addition, Hollywood films seemed to show that the Indian and the buffalo shared the same end, that they were of the past and were no more.

Holston Treaty,

signed in 1791, put into place another agreement between the United States and the Cherokee. This agreement, just six years after the Hopewell Treaty, again put pressure on the Cherokee to give up territory. The U.S. set the new northern border at Holston,

Tennessee. The treaty banned nonnative people from settling on Cherokee land, promised federal protection of the Cherokees, and returned native prisoners. In return, the U.S. received rights to build a road through their territory, use the Tennessee River, and control all trade with the Cherokee. The Holston Treaty lasted until 1835, when the Cherokee signed the Treaty of New Echota.

Honey Springs, Oklahoma, was the

site of the largest Civil War battle in Indian Territory. The South had 5,000 Cherokee, Creek, Chickasaw, Choctaw, and Texans led by Brigadier General Douglas H. Cooper. The North had 3,000 Cherokee, Creek, African Americans, and soldiers under the leadership of General James G. Blunt. Though outnumbered, the North had more artillery than the South, who only had howitzers. In July 1863, after a rainy night, the two sides clashed. The South's damp gunpowder made their weapons misfire. With Blunt's troops coming on strong with heavy artillery, Cooper ordered a retreat. As they retreated, they burned the supplies they could not take with them. With this win, the North positioned itself to take control of Indian Territory. Native peoples in Indian Territory only wanted to keep their land and survive. The South's defeat at Honey Springs resulted in many native peoples switching sides to join the North.

Hooker Jim (about 1825-1879 (also

known as Hooka) was a Modoc chief during the Modoc War in the Oregon-California border region. Captain Jack, another Modoc chief, and his followers left their assigned reservation due to poor conditions and mistreatment. After an attack on Hooker Jim by settlers, he and his people responded by killing 12 of them. On the run, they joined Captain Jack's group in late 1872 in an area called the lava beds. The U.S. Army failed to blast the Modoc out of their position and attempted peace talks. In April 1873, General Edward Canby and four others approached the tribe. The Modoc killed General Canby and one other and injured a third. Hooker Jim regretted having agreed to the murders, for the killings increased the army's determination to beat the Modoc and force them onto a reservation. Hooker Jim made a separate peace agreement allowing him and his family to go to Indian Territory.

See also: Modoc War

WORDS TO KNOW

artillery (ar-TIHL-er-ee): cannons and other big guns used in warfare

howitzer (HOW-iht-ser): a piece of short-range artillery favored by cavalry units because it was easy to move and could be positioned quickly

manpower (MAN-pow-er): the number of people that could be put to work

Hopi (also known as Moqui or Moki) comes from the word Hopituh, meaning *the peaceful ones*. The Hopi, a Pueblo people descended from the ancient Anasazi, located their villages on First, Second, and Third Mesas, all part of the region known as Black Mesa in northeastern Arizona. Traditional Hopi homes look similar to apartments. They crafted the walls of stones and cemented them in place with adobe, a kind of mud plaster. Log beams formed the roof, and cracks and spaces were filled in with branches, leaves, grass, and more adobe. The homes had no doors or windows. People entered through a hole in the roof and climbed down a ladder into the room.

This Hopi girl at Walpi in 1900 has a traditional squash blossom hairstyle showing she is ready for marriage.

Hopi people still live at Walpi, Arizona.

The Hopi dug underground worship rooms called kivas. They believed the kiva to be an entrance to the underworld, the place from where Hopi ancestors first rose to live on the Earth.

Their remote location protected the Hopi from Europeans until the 1500s. Spanish explorer Coronado and his men reached them in 1540. In 1598, Spaniard Juan de Oñate and his soldiers conquered the villages and enslaved the people. When the Spanish outlawed kachinas, the normally peaceful Hopi fought to regain their homeland by taking part in the Pueblo Rebellion in 1680. The Hopi avoided most of the Indian wars of the 1800s. However, in 1887 the government built a boarding school at Keams Canyon, Arizona, and forced Hopi children to attend. Also during this time, smallpox first came to the Hopi and many died.

The Hopi today have one of the most unchanged cultures of all Native Americans. Their traditional villages still sit on the three mesas. They continue to shape their lives around peaceful living and forgiveness, the Hopi Way.

FACT FILE

Language: The Hopi speak a Uto-Aztecan language, unlike other Pueblo people.

Location: They live in northern Arizona, part of the Southwest Culture Area.

Diet: They hunted deer, antelope, rabbits, and other game animals, planted squash, beans, and corn, their most important crop, and gathered wild edible plants and roots.

Kachinas, or katsinam, play an important role in many ceremonies. They are guardian spirits said to live among the people for half the year.

Interesting Fact: Kachinas represent natural elements, like rain and animals, but also ideas like discipline and honor. Parents teach their children about the hundreds of different kachinas through kachina dolls. The children do not play with the dolls, but instead learn their stories and treat them with respect.

Hopi and Navajo Relocation Act

of 1974, also called the Navajo-Hopi Land Settlement Act, refers to a law dividing shared Hopi and Navajo lands and requiring the removal of about 12,000 Navajo from the Hopi share and 100 Hopi from the Navajo share. Supporters of the act claimed it would settle land use disputes between the two tribes. Those against the act saw it as a sneaky way for tribal councils to lease the rights to mine billions of dollars worth of coal from the Black Mesa area.

The United States Department of the Interior created tribal councils in the 1920s as a way to help mining companies gain access to reservation lands. The Bureau of Indian Affairs permitted the tribal councils to approve mineral leases. Traditionally, Navajo clans made decisions concerning the tribe. Because the Hopi and the Navajo shared the land, the mining companies were uncertain which tribe could legally lease it to them. By passing the act, the government cleared the way. To encourage people to leave their homeland, the law also outlawed the construction and repair of buildings and the upkeep of roads.

The Navajos compare the removal to the Cherokee Trail of Tears in the 1800s. Of the families who did move, many lost their independent way of living. In 2005, with a few hundred Navajo still refusing to leave and the relocation of others being called a disaster, some members of Congress tried to make changes to the law, but the changes failed to pass.

Horn bowl refers to a polished bowl or container made from the horn of a sheep, bison, or other horned animal. The Haida, a band of native people living on the Queen Charlotte Islands off the coast of British Columbia, Canada, crafted horn bowls from sheep.

Horses arrived in North America with Spanish explorers invading from the south. Horses spread throughout the Plains region to nearly every tribe by the mid-1700s. Tribes recognized the value of horses and traded for them or raided them from neighboring tribes and settlements. Horses changed the Plains peoples from a mostly farming way of life to a culture centered on hunting bison herds. The communities could now travel to far away places, following the herds that provided them with food, clothing, and shelter, and furs to trade for other goods. Prior to horses, many tribes used dogs to pull loads. They could not carry as much as a horse, and unlike horses that grazed grass when hungry, dogs ate meat so they were harder to keep fed. Children learned to ride at a young age, and the tribe expected and prized excellent horsemanship. Tribe members practiced battle moves while riding, such as learning to shoot arrows from different positions. They also held races for sport. Often they rode bareback or with just a simple pad saddled on the horse.

Spanish conquerors brought the Colonial Spanish horse, also known as the Spanish mustang, to the New World.

Native American carvings and ceremonial objects reflect the importance horses had in Native American cultures.

Horseshoe Bend refers to the March 1814 battle during the War of 1812. General Andrew Jackson led 3,300 troops against about 1,000 Upper Creek warriors, also called the Red Sticks, in a fight over land possession. Chief Menawa led the Creek defense. Over 800 warriors died, making the battle the bloodiest in United States history for First Peoples. The Red Sticks killed or wounded about 200 of Jackson's troops. In August 1814, the tribe's remaining people surrendered to Jackson and shortly after signed the Treaty of Fort Jackson, giving up over 20 million acres (over 8 million hectares) of their land to the United States. This represented over half their holdings. In part, General Jackson's victory over the Upper Creek led to his election as president of the United States in 1829. During his term, he signed into law the Indian Removal Act, forcing all Native Americans east of the Mississippi to move to Oklahoma.

See also: Jackson, Andrew

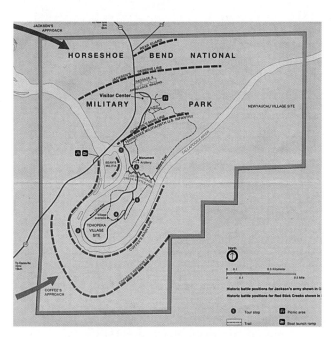

Horseshoe Bend takes its name after a part of Alabama's Tallapoosa River. Gray lines show battle positions for Jackson's army, while purple lines show battle positions for the Red Sticks.

A Native American statue by Allan Houser called "May We Have Peace" stands on Oklahoma University's grounds.

Houser, Allan (1914-1994), born Allan Haozous on a farm in Oklahoma, was a talented Chiricahua Apache artist. His paintings and sculptures offered an understanding of Native American culture and the traditional daily life of Apache families. He also sculpted figures in bronze, marble, and wood. He taught in art schools in the United States, including the Institute of American Indian Arts in Santa Fe, New Mexico. After retiring from teaching in 1975, he created over 1,000 sculptures, working in his studio up to his death in 1994. In 1992, he received the National Medal of the Arts from President George W. Bush to celebrate and honor his life's work.

Howard, Oliver O.

(1830-1909) was a military leader, diplomat, and a religious man with a strong sense of right and wrong. He attended the United States Military Academy at West Point. He served as a Union general in the Civil War. After the war he headed the Freedman's Bureau, a government agency created to help former slaves. He founded an all-black college in the District of Columbia, which was later named after him. In 1872, President Grant sent him west to meet with Chiricahua Apache leader Cochise in an attempt to end the Apache warfare against settlers. He negotiated a successful treaty by promising the Apaches that they could choose their reservation lands. In 1877, Howard was commanded to go to Oregon and move the Nez Perce people to a reservation set aside for them in Idaho. Though he agreed with Nez Perce tribal leader, Chief Joseph, that the Nez Perce had never signed a treaty giving up their homeland, he felt bound to his army orders. He led troops against Chief Joseph and his people in the Nez Perce War until their surrender. After retiring from the military in 1894, Howard wrote several books about his life experiences.

See also: Cochise and Joseph, Chief

Howe, LeAnne

(1951-), of Choctaw heritage, writes books, poems, and plays about the Native American experience. She grew up in Oklahoma and received her advanced education from Oklahoma State University and Vermont College. In 2002, her first book, *Shell Shaker*, received an American Book Award from the Before Columbus Foundation and a Wordcraft Circle Writer of the Year award. A book of poetry, *Evidence of Red*, received an Oklahoma Book Award in 2006. She teaches at the college level, and has worked to push colleges to encourage Native Americans to attend and complete their college degrees.

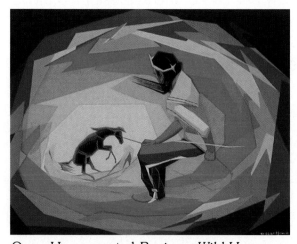

Oscar Howe created *Roping a Wild Horse*.

Howe, Oscar

(1915-1983), a Yanktonai Sioux artist, was born on the Crow Creek Indian Reservation in South Dakota. His grandmother, Shell Face, taught him the traditional stories and culture of his ancestors. In 1935, he attended the Santa Fe Indian School and joined its new art program. After graduating, the South Dakota Artist Project hired him to paint murals in Mitchell and Mobridge. He served in the United States Army in World War II, then attended the Dakota Wesleyan University and served in its arts department. He later joined the faculty at the University of South Dakota and taught art, while continuing to work on his own award-winning paintings. Howe's work was honored fifteen times with the Waite Phillips Trophy for Outstanding Contributions to American Indian Art. Museums all over the world show and collect his work.

Hualapai (also known as Walapai, meaning *people of the tall pine*) refers to a tribe that lives among the piñon trees that dot their mountainous homeland in northwestern Arizona. They wore leather clothing in warm weather, and added rabbit skin blankets and robes in winter. Spiritual healers cared for the ill and led their religious practices, which focused on gods and demons from an unseen world. The Hualapai traded with the nearby Hopi and Mojave. Spanish explorers reached them in the 1500s, but did not settle among them, likely because of the poor farming prospects and general lack of material wealth. In the 1850s, mining outfits in the area hired the natives. Because of cruel treatment, the Hualapai fought back. Troops and nonnative miners crushed the rebellion by burning Hualapai homes and crops. In 1874, the government forced the Hualapai to live on the Mojave reservation, and in 1883, they received a reservation of their own. Today the tribe of about 1,500 people supports itself through timber sales, fishing, cattle ranching, farming, hunting, and Grand Canyon tourism.

FACT FILE

Location: They live in the mountains of northwestern Arizona.

Diet: Because of the dry climate, the Hualapai hunted deer, rabbits, and antelope, fished in the Colorado River, and gathered wild plant foods, like piñon nuts and cactus fruit, for most of their food needs. They farmed when and where water was available.

Housing: The Hualapai built domed shelters of poles, brush, grass, and earth. While out looking for food, they used temporary brush shelters.

Edward Curtis photographed this Hualapai winter camp in 1907.

Hudson's Bay Company or HBC,

was a British fur trading company officially started in 1670 in today's Canada at Hudson Bay, an important shipping route. Prince Rupert, cousin of King Charles II, convinced the king to support a fur trading business in the New World. The king agreed and granted the company sole trading rights in lands crossed by any river flowing into Hudson Bay. This huge territory was named Rupert's Land. The first ships left England in 1668. HBC built forts at the mouths of rivers on Hudson Bay as trading posts.

The fur trade nearly extinguished North America's beaver population.

The trade of animal furs and hides dominated the economy of North America for hundreds of years. The French and British valued furs, and North America provided a wealthy resource.

Since they had no competition, HBC made large profits until the late 1740s. First Peoples provided the labor; they

harvested the animals, prepared the furs, and delivered them to the trading post. In exchange, they received tools, cloth, blankets, beads, mirrors, metal pots, guns and ammunition, and other goods. Aboriginal peoples came to depend on these goods.

In the 1800s, the fur trade declined. The fashions changed in Europe; now most stylish people wore silk hats. Less expensive furs coming out of South America took the place of North American furs. And all the trapping and hunting had reduced the number of animals left to harvest. In order to stay in business, HBC began to sell land to farmers and developers and also sell them supplies. In the late 1800s, it changed from a company of trading posts to one of modern stores. In the first half of the 1900s it developed coal, oil, and natural gas interests. In 1991, HBC got out of the fur business altogether. Today, Canada's oldest company is a large, successful chain of stores.

WORDS TO KNOW

Aboriginal (ab-uh-RIH-jihn-uhl): the first people in an area

extinction (ek-STINGKT-shuhn): the loss of all living members of a life form, or species

hides (HIDZ): the skins or pelts of animals

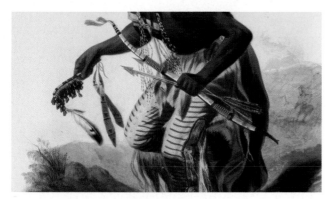

Hundreds of years before the introduction of guns, tribes used bows and arrows for hunting.

Hunting

Hunting animals provided native people with high-energy food, hides for making clothing and trading, and horns and bones for making tools, jewelry, and containers. Depending on where the tribe was located and what they were hunting, weapons varied. Coastal hunters often used harpoons or spears and nets, while inland hunters used bows and arrows, spears, and traps. Plains peoples worked together on bison hunts. One effective way to kill enough meat for the entire tribe was to stampede a bison herd off a tall cliff.

The introduction of guns and horses made hunting easier. Native peoples could harvest more animals than they needed to eat, and because of this, they were able to trade for more European goods. This led them to a different way of life, one more dependent on the land's animal resources and more dependent on the goods for which they traded. The Plains tribes came to depend so much on hunting bison that it became a point of weakness. In the mid-1800s, when soldiers, western settlers, and native peoples hunted bison to near extinction, many tribes suffered.

Hupa (also known as Hoopa) shared similar cultures with their neighbors, the Karuk, or Karok, and Yurok peoples. The Hupa name comes from the Yurok name for the valley in which they live, Hoopa Valley. They hunted, fished, and gathered wild plant foods. They ground acorns to make flour from which they made bread, porridge, and other foods. Like the Northwest Coast peoples, the Hupa built red cedar canoes and homes. The homes sheltered them from the wet, cool winters and dry summers. They made their clothing from buckskin. Elders taught traditional skills such as basket weaving.

In 1864, the United States government set aside the Hoopa Valley as a reservation for the Hupa, the largest reservation in California. Today they number about 2,600 people. They continue many of their traditions and support themselves through farming, forest industries, raising livestock, and a casino.

The Hupa performed World Renewal dances including the White Deerskin Dance.

Huron (also called Wyandot, Wyandotte, Wendat, or Guyandot) means *rough* in French, possibly referring to the men's bristly hairstyle. They used canoes, and dogs helped carry their belongings on land. Huron society organized itself by clan. The Huron trapped furs for the French. The Iroquois nations trapped for the Dutch and British. Overhunting caused the Iroquois tribes to push into Huron lands. Years of war with the Iroquois nations and European disease killed off about half their people. In 1649, the Iroquois nations chased them from their land. Those not adopted by the Iroquois tribes escaped to Quebec in Canada, the Great Lakes, and later Kansas and Oklahoma, where reservations exist today.

FACT FILE

Language: They spoke an Iroquoian language called Wyandot, also known as Huron-Wendat.

Location: They originally lived in the Northeast Culture Area in a part of Ontario, Canada, between Lake Simcoe and Georgian Bay.

Diet: They ate deer, turkeys, rabbits, nuts, berries, and raised crops of squash, beans, corn, and tobacco.

Housing: They built longhouses, stretching up to 150 feet (46 meters) long and sheltering as many as 60 people.

Customs: They valued wampum, the tiny purple or white shell beads used to make ceremonial belts.

Igaluk (also known as Aningan) is the powerful Inuit god of the moon. In Inuit mythology, Igaluk and his sister Malina lived in the same village. After Igaluk treated her cruelly, she ran into the night carrying a torch. Igaluk ran after her, but his torch dimmed, leaving only a glowing ember. As they ran, the wind swept them into the sky. Igaluk became the moon while Malina, with her bright light, became the sun.

Igloo builders shaped blocks for a perfect fit.

Igloo, a traditional Inuit snowhouse, provides warm shelter in snowy, treeless areas. The Central Inuit cut blocks of packed snow and set them in a circle to form the house's base. They then added more blocks to form a dome and carefully sealed off drafts. Inside the igloo, body warmth raised the air temperature to a comfortable 50 to 60° Fahrenheit (10 to 15° Celsius). In Greenland, the native people made ice shelters large enough for sports competitions and community events.

Iglulik snowhouse, built by the Iglulik band of Inuit, is similar to the igloos built by other Inuit people. During the winter, they lined the shelter with sealskins to supply additional warmth and comfort. Stone lamps filled with animal oil provided heat and fuel for cooking inside the snowhouse. The Iglulik built snowhouses with open tops roofed with sealskin in the summer.

Illinois (also known as Ilaniawaki, Illinik, or more recently, Illini meaning *the people*) lived far enough west to use both prairie and woodland resources. Men hunted and fished. Women farmed and gathered wild foods. Men sometimes crowned their heads with feather wreaths and wore necklaces made from woven bison fur, deer hair tassels, small metal cones, porcupine quills, and feathers. War, disease, and assimilation caused a population decline from 10,000 people in the 1670s to about 300 people in 1832.

FACT FILE

Language: The Illinois spoke an Algonquian language.

Location: They occupied a large territory south of Wisconsin in the Mississippi River Valley, including parts of the today's states of Iowa, Illinois, Missouri, and Arkansas.

Diet: Main foods included bison, deer, fish, maple sap, berries, nuts, fruits, crops of corn, beans, squash, pumpkins, and watermelon.

Housing: They sheltered in longhouses in the summer and wigwams in the winter.

Customs: They believed in one supreme god, the creator Kitchesmanetoa. They also honored the sun and thunder, which they thought of as part of Kitchesmanetoa.

Interesting Fact: Hunters lit a circle of fire around a bison herd, except for one small opening. When the animals tried to escape the flames by running through the opening, the hunters would shoot them.

Illinois Confederacy,

made up of many Illinois tribes, shared a language and a similar lifestyle. Over time, these tribes joined together or separated according to their needs. In the 1700s, five main bands of people formed the Illinois, including Cahokia, Kaskaskia, Michigamea, Peoria, and Tamaroa. By the early 1830s, the tribal confederacy had dissolved under pressure from war and disease, and only two tribes remained. The Kaskaskia and Peoria left their homeland in Illinois State and settled on reservations, first in Kansas, then in Oklahoma.

Incising

pottery as a method of decoration requires a steady hand. To incise, the potter cuts lines and patterns into the object's surface before the object is heated, or fired. The designs cut deeply enough to show, but not so deep that the pottery weakens or the cuts break through the clay wall. Ancient and modern Native American artists create incised pottery, including the Oneota, Creek, Apalachee, and Tomé.

The artist incised owl kachinas and patterns into this vessel.

Indian

refers to the name given to the first peoples living in North America. Humans first populated North America about 14,000 years ago after the last Ice Age. European explorers met these Aboriginal North Americans when they sailed west in search of a new water route to India and the Far East. When they reached North America, they believed they had reached India and called the peoples Indians. Today, native people may prefer the name First Nations, a term especially used in Canada, First Peoples, Native Americans, or Aboriginal people.

In Canada, Indian is a legal term used in laws and agreements between the government and those bands that are not Inuit or Métis. Métis are descendents of both Europeans and Aboriginal peoples.

Indian Appropriations Act

of 1871 stated that the United States government would no longer consider any tribe to be a separate nation. This meant that the federal government would no longer sign treaties with tribes. This act took power away from tribal governments and made tribes dependents of the United States. Congress repealed the act in 1934 in an effort to revitalize tribal culture and government. They replaced it with the Indian Reorganization Act.

See also: Indian Reorganization Act of 1934

In the Carlisle School's tin shop, students learned practical skills.

Indian boarding schools were a

part of the United States' plan to civilize Native Americans, erase their cultures and languages, and make their young people accept and live the culture of people of European descent. In 1891, Congress required attendance of all Indian children of school age. The Carlisle School and the Hampton Institute were two of the best known, although Indian schools opened across the country. The instructors gave the children European-style clothing and hairstyles and taught them English reading, writing, and speech. Students gained skills in housekeeping, typing, sewing, factory work, and farming. Students who spoke their home language received punishments. Homesick and miserable, exposed to disease and cruelty, many children did not survive. A few of the most capable children took the best the schools had to offer and did more than survive. They learned to read and write and used those skills for the benefit of their people after they left the schools.

See also: Carlisle School and Hampton Institute

Indian Cavalry joined the fighting in

the American Civil War in Indian Territory in Oklahoma. Most Native Americans sided with the South, including the Choctaw, Chickasaw, Seminole, Cherokee, and Creek. Indian Territory, between the South's Texas and the North's Kansas, became highly desired land. Native American fighters were looking for the best way to survive the war with their culture and land rights unchanged.

Indian Claims Commission Act

See General Allotment Act

Indian Gaming Regulatory Act,

passed by Congress in 1988, provides rules on Native American tribal gaming, or gambling. Gaming, a traditional part of Native American cultures, has dramatically changed many reservations for the better. In the 1980s, tribes began to use gambling businesses as a way to bring needed money into the reservations. States demanded control over gambling businesses within their borders. Tribes claimed freedom from state rule. The Indian Gaming Regulatory Act serves as a compromise between tribes and states and describes their roles regarding gambling.

WORDS TO KNOW

civilize (SIH-vuh-lize): to assimilate into nonnative ways of living

regulatory (REH-gew-lah-tor-ee): intended to control something

Indian Removal Act of 1830

allowed the U.S. president to make removal treaties with tribes living east of the Mississippi River. By the 1830s, southern states hungered for more land to expand the booming cotton business. They pressured southeastern tribes to give up their lands. President Andrew Jackson wanted to move all tribes to Indian Territory. Under the act, tribes received land in the West for their eastern lands. Those individuals not willing to move became citizens of their home state. These new citizens often faced mistreatment from settlers. In addition, when entire nations fought removal, Jackson forced them to leave. By 1837, almost 50,000 Native American people had been removed from about 25 million acres (over 10 million hectares) of land.

See also: Jackson, Andrew and Trail of Tears

After only one year in office, President Andrew Jackson pushed the Indian Removal Act into law.

Indian Reorganization Act of 1934,

also known as the Wheeler-Howard Act, tried to repair some of the damage done by the Indian Appropriations Act of 1871 and the General Allotment Act of 1887. The act gave tribes back the right to self-rule and moved to protect and develop tribal lands for the benefit of the tribe. It also provided for a loan system, job training, and education of Native Americans. Though still in effect today, some Native Americans find the act offensive, because it treats them as children or dependents of the state.

See also: General Allotment Act and Indian Appropriations Act of 1871

WORDS TO KNOW

act (AKT): a bill passed by Congress which can become a law when it is signed by the president

offensive (uh-FEHN-sihv): hurtful or insulting; disrespectful

Indian Reserve

is land set aside for use by Aboriginal peoples in Canada by the Canadian government. The Indian bands do not own the land, but may live on it and use it for their benefit. Americans use the term reservation.

Indian Territory officially established in 1830s, provided a new homeland for many Native American tribes. The United States government sent many tribes living east of the Mississippi River to Indian Territory under the Indian Removal Act of 1830. These tribes included the Five Civilized Tribes, or the Cherokee, Muskogee or Creek, Choctaw, Chickasaw, and Seminole, and also the Eastern Shawnee, Seneca-Cayuga, Wyandotte, Peoria, Modoc, Quapaw, Ottawa, and Miami peoples in the eastern half of the territory. In the western part of the territory lived many more tribes, including the Osage, Sac and Fox, Iowa, Kickapoo, Caddo, Wichita, Delaware, Kaw, Ponca, Tonkawa, Cheyenne, Arapaho, Kiowa, Comanche, Pawnee, Otoe, Missouria, and Apache. Later, the United States split the territory and named the western part Oklahoma Territory and the eastern part Indian Territory. Together, they became the state of Oklahoma in 1907.

See also: Indian Removal Act

This map shows the flow of Indian Removal to Indian Territory.

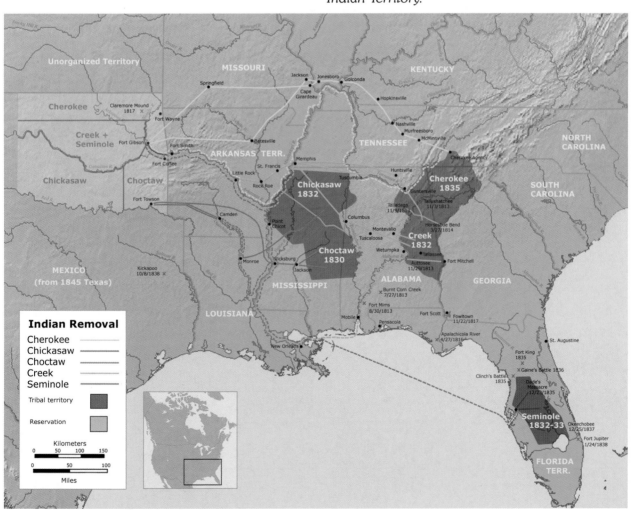

The American Indian is of the soil, whether it be the region of forests, plains, pueblos, or mesas. He fits into the landscape, for the hand that fashioned the continent also fashioned the man for his surroundings. He once grew as naturally as the wild sunflowers, he belongs just as the buffalo belonged....

Luther Standing Bear, Oglala Sioux
1868-1939

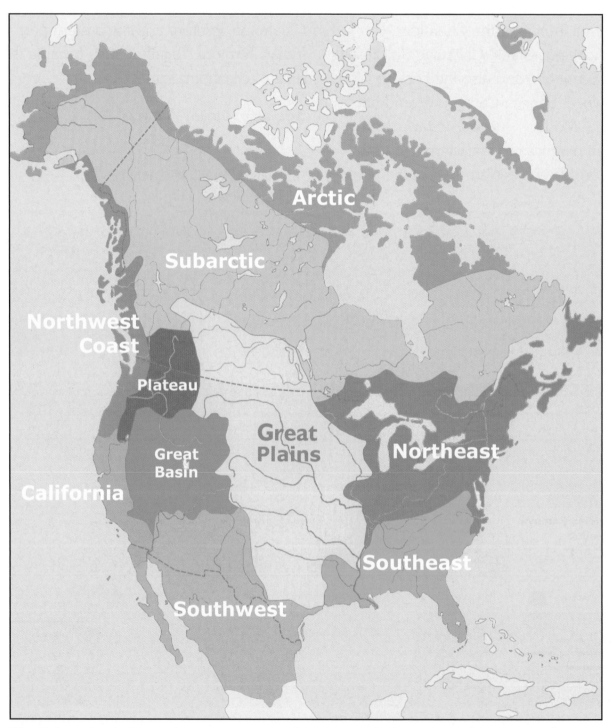

The Culture Areas shown above are one way of categorizing Indian peoples by culture and geography. See page 55 for lists of tribes in each Culture Area.

Tribes Organized by Culture Areas

ARCTIC CULTURE AREA

(Arctic Peoples)
Aleut
Inuit

CALIFORNIA CULTURE AREA

(California Indians)
Achomawi (Pit River Indians)
Cahuilla
Chimariko
Chumash
Costanoan
Cupeño
Diegueño (Tipai-Ipai)
Esselen
Gabrieleño
Hupa
Karok
Luiseño
Maidu
Miwok
Pomo
Salinas
Shasta
Tolowa
Wintun
Yahi
Yokuts
Yuki
Yurok

GREAT BASIN CULTURE AREA

(Great Basin Indians)
Bannock
Paiute
Shoshone
Ute
Washoe

GREAT PLAINS CULTURE AREA

(Plains Indians)
Arapaho
Arikara
Assiniboine
Blackfeet
Cheyenne
Comanche
Crow
Gros Ventre (Atsina)
Hidatsa
Ioway
Kaw
Kiowa
Mandan
Missouria
Omaha
Osage
Otoe
Pawnee
Ponca
Quapaw
Sarcee
Sioux (Dakota, Lakota, Nakota)
Tonkawa
Wichita

NORTHEAST CULTURE AREA

(Northeast Indians)
Abenaki
Algonkin
Ojibwe (Ojibway, Chippewa)
Erie
Huron (Wyandot)
Illinois
Iroquois (Haudenosaunee)
  Cayuga
  Mohawk
  Oneida
  Onondaga
  Seneca
  Tuscarora
Kickapoo
Lenni Lenape (Delaware)
Mahican
Maliseet
Massachuset
Menominee
Meskwaki (Fox)
Miami
Micmac
Mohegan
Montauk
Nanticoke
Narragansett
Neutral
Niantic
Nipmuc
Ottawa
Passamaquoddy
Pennacook
Penobscot
Pequot
Potawatomi
Powhatan
Roanoke
Sac
Shawnee
Susquehannock
Tionontati
Wampanoag
Wappinger
Winnebago (Ho-Chunk)

NORTHWEST COAST CULTURE AREA

(Northwest Coast Indians)
Bella Coola
Chinook
Coos
Cowichan
Duwamish
Haida
Kalapuya
Kwakiutl
Makah
Nisqually
Nootka
Puyallup
Quileute
Quinault
Squaxon
Takelma
Tlingit
Tsimishian
Umpqua
Yaquina

PLATEAU CULTURE AREA

(Plateau Indians)
Cayuse
Coeur d'Alene
Columbia (Sinkiuse)
Flathead
Kalispel
Klamath
Klickitat
Kootenai
Modoc
Nez Perce
Ntlakyapamuk (Thompson)
Okanagan (Sinaietk)
Palouse
Umatilla
Spokan
Stuwihamuk
Walla Walla
Wanapam
Wishram
Yakama

SOUTHEAST CULTURE AREA

(Southeast Indians)
Alabama
Apalachee
Atakapa
Caddo
Calusa
Catawba
Chitimacha
Choctaw
Coushatta
Creek
Lumbee
Mobile
Natchez
Seminole
Shakori
Timucua
Tunica
Yamasee
Yazoo
Yuchi

SOUTHWEST CULTURE AREA

(Southwest Indians)
Akimel O'odham (Pima)
Apache
Coahuiltec
Havasupai
Hopi
Hualapai
Karankawa
Keres
Mojave
Navajo
Pueblo Indians
Tewa
Tiwa
Tohono O'odham (Papago)
Towa (Jemez)
Yaqui
Yavapai
Yuma (Quechan)
Zuni

SUBARCTIC CULTURE AREA

(Subarctic Indians)
Ahtena
Beaver (Tsattine)
Beothuk
Carrier (Dakelh)
Chipewyan
Ojibwe (Chippewa) *(most Ojibwe bands part of Northeast Culture Area)*
Cree
Dogrib (Thlingchadinne)
Han
Hare (Kawchotinne)
Koyukon
Kutchin
Montagnais
Naskapi
Slavey (Etchareottine)
Tanaina
Tanana
Yellowknife (Tatsanottine)

Raven Brings Light to the World

Adapted from a Haida Legend

Illustrated by Charles Reasoner

Long ago before there were stars, a moon, or even the sun, the Earth was dark and all the animals and people lived without any kind of light.

Raven had dark, purple and black feathers which blended in perfectly with the darkness around him. He would perch on cedar branches and carefully watch everything around him with his coal black eyes.

Except for his voice, "Kaw! Kaw!" You wouldn't even know he was there, watching. Turning his head, first this way, then that. Always watching.
"Kaw! Kaw!"

Now Raven was the smartest of all birds and some said he was the smartest of all the animals. By carefully watching the people and animals, Raven had learned to act like them and sometimes even look like them! Raven liked to think he was the smartest of all.

One day, while Raven was busy watching from his favorite branch, he spied an old man carrying a wooden box into the woods.

"Curious," thought Raven. "I should see what he is up too." Raven hopped from branch to branch and followed the old man into the forest.

When he thought he was alone, the old man slowly opened the box and brilliant light shot out in every direction, lighting the forest around them! Raven nearly fell off his branch!

"Kaw!" he thought to himself. "What a wondrous thing! I must have that light!"

The old man, thinking someone might be watching, quickly put the lid back on the box, tucked it under his arm, and hurried back to the village. The old man guarded the box carefully and never went anywhere without it.

Raven followed silently thinking about the beautiful light he had seen.

It just so happened that the old man had a beautiful daughter and a young grandson who were the delight of his old age.

Both of them had coal black hair and their eyes twinkled in a special way when they were together.

None of this escaped Raven's watchful eyes.

The small child had shiny black hair and eyes just like Raven.

"This will be easy!" thought Raven.

The old man loved his young grandson very much and would do anything for his happiness. One day when he was gathering berries he heard his grandson calling for him.

"Grandfather! Grandfather, where are you?"

Knowing his grandson should not be alone in the forest, the old man answered, "Over here. Come to my voice!"

When the old man saw his grandson he seemed different somehow. His hair was shiny black and his eyes gleamed. When the boy spoke his voice sounded different too.

"Kaw! Kaw!" said the boy. "Please let me see into your magic box grandfather. Kaw-please?"

"What is wrong with your voice, grandson? You sound different," said the old man clinging tightly to his wooden box.

The boy pleaded, "It is just a Kaw-cough, grandfather! Please let me just look into your magic box one time."

At first the old man said no, but finally gave into the boy. The old man slowly removed the lid from the box and white light spilled into the world.

The young boy picked up the round, shiny light and instantly turned into Raven!

"Kaw! Kaw! Kaw!" said Raven as he flew higher and higher into the air carrying the bright light in his shiny black beak. Higher he flew until the light became the sun and it is still there today!

That is how clever Raven, the smartest of all the animals, brought light into the world.

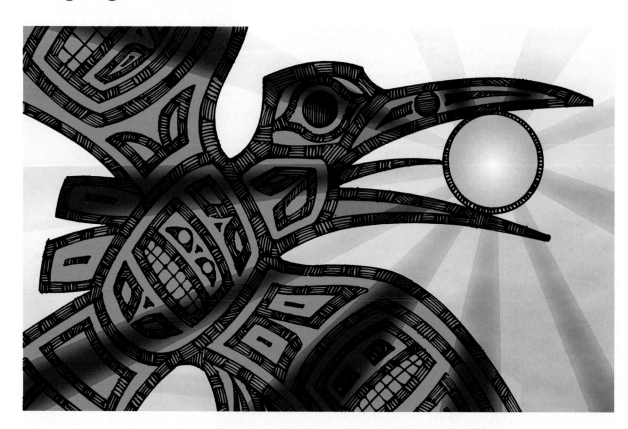

HOW DO I SAY IT?

Fox (FAHKS)

Gabrieleño (gab-ree-eh-LAY-nyoh)

Great Basin Indians (GRAYT BAY-sihn IN-dee-ihnz)

Great Plains Indians (GRAYT PLAYNZ IN-dee-ihnz)

Gros Ventre (GROW VAHN-truh)

Hackensack (HAK-uhn-sak)

Haida (HI-duh)

Han (HAHN)

Hare (HAIR)

Havasupai (hah-vah-SOO-pie)

Hidatsa (hee-DOT-suh)

Hohokam (ho-HO-kum)

Hopi (HO-pee)

Hualapai (WAH-lah-pie)

Hupa (HOO-puh)

Huron (HYUR-on)

Illinois (ill-uh-NOY)